Sounds Like Alberta

(1754 - 1905)

Colin A. Thomson and F. Lee Prindle

DETSELIG
ENTERPRISES LTD

Calgary, Alberta

Sounds Like Alberta

Library and Archives Canada Cataloguing in Publication

Thomson, Colin A., 1938-
    Sounds Like Alberta: 1754-1905 / Colin A. Thomson and F. Lee Prindle.

Includes bibliographical references and index.
ISBN-13: 978-155059-310-5
ISBN-10: 1-55059-310-2

1. Alberta--Biography. I. Prindle, F.Lee, 1937- II. Title.

FC3217.T46 2006   971.23'009'9   C2006-900409-9

Detselig Enterprises Ltd.
210, 1220 Kensington Road NW
Calgary, Alberta
T2N 3P5

www.temerondetselig.com
Email: temeron@telusplanet.net
Phone: (403) 283-0900
Fax: (403) 283-6947

We acknowledge the support of the Government of Canada through the Book Publishing Industry Development Program (BPIDP) for our publishing program.

We also acknowledge the support of the Alberta Foundation for the Arts for our publishing program.

SAN 113-0234
ISBN 1-55059-310-2   978-1-55059-310-5
Front cover photo by T.E. Giles   Back cover photo by Sonia Gonsalves
Printed in Canada   *Cover Design by Alvin Choong*

Dedication

The authors dedicate this book to Eleanor Thomson, Lucelle Prindle and Rona Thompson for their assistance and support

Table of Contents

Introduction 7

Part I – Noteworthy Voices 9
  Anthony Henday 9
  Peter Pond 13
  Peter Fidler 15
  David Thompson 18
  Daniel Williams Harmon 23
  Sir George Simpson 25
  John Rowand 30
  John Palliser 33
  "Twelve Foot" Davis 36
  James Carnegie, Earl of Southesk 38
  John Macoun 42
  Walter Butler Cheadle 44
  William Francis Butler 48
  Jerry Potts 51
  George "Kootenai" Brown 56

Part II – Words from Notable Groups 61
  Aboriginal Voices: Quotes from and about the
    first Albertans 61
      Crowfoot (Isapo-Muxika) 68
      Swift Runner 74
  Minority Voices 79
      Blacks 80
      John Ware 82
      Jesse Williams 85
      Chinese 87

  The Law and Outlaws 89
      James Farquharson Macleod 94
      Cecil E. Denny 98

  Missionaries and Church Leaders 102
      Albert Lacombe 106
      Charles Ora Card 112
      John McDougall 115

Part III – Settlements and Vistas 119
    The Sound of Edmonton 126
    At Fort Chipewyan 129
    The Sound of Calgary   130
    Small Town Alberta Buildings 132
    The Sounds of Transportation 132

Part IV – *Expressions* 137
    Booze 137
    Sounds of the Hunters, Trappers and Traders 139
    Characters and Pioneer Humor 141
    Fort Macleod Hotel Rules 145
    Pioneer Women 146
    A Pioneer School Teacher 151
    Silence of Death 152
    Political Voices   154
    Sir Frederick William Haultain 156

Part V – *Alberta Particulars* 159
    What's in a Name 159
    Alberta Vernacular 1880s Style 161
    Alberta Timeline to 1905 162

Bibliography 167

Index 173

Introduction

In 1754 Anthony Henday, an employee of the Hudson Bay Company, became the first known European to visit Alberta and view the Rocky Mountains.

One hundred and fifty-one years later on September 1, 1905, the day the Province of Alberta was born, Prime Minister Wilfrid Laurier spoke to a celebrating audience in Edmonton:

> We do not anticipate, nor do we want, that any individual should forget the land of their origin or their ancestors. Let them look to the past, but let them also look to the future; Let them look to the land of their ancestors, but let them look also to the land of their children.
> (*The Formation of Alberta*)

During the century and a half between 1754 and 1905, many other comments from and about Alberta and its people were recorded. From these, the authors chose statements and observations that spoke of the grandeur, passion, danger, hardship, hatred, violence, fear, humor, commitment, love, optimism, and raw courage that were part of Alberta's history.

Some topics naturally overlap and in such situations, the authors made an editorial choice on where specific items were placed, aware that many items could fit in more than one section.

In some instances, the reader will find different spellings of the same word as the authors tried to be true to the sources. Some examples are: Athabasca, Athabaska; Whiskey, Whisky; Klondike, Klondyke; Piegan, Peigan; and Stoney, Stony. Other misspellings also in preservation of the original documents.

Unless otherwise noted, *Alberta* refers to the area that now constitutes the province.

The opinions expressed in this book do not necessarily reflect those of the authors but are included for historical reasons.

About the Authors

Colin Thomson, a seventh generation Canadian, was raised in rural Saskatchewan. He is a Professor Emeritus at the University of Lethbridge. He has served universities in Edmonton, Saskatoon, Kenya, Lesotho, and Nigeria. He and his wife, Eleanor, reside in a home overlooking the Oldman River with a beautiful view of the Rocky Mountains. He loves to write and this is his tenth book (his second in collaboration with Lee Prindle).

F. Lee Prindle is retired from Lethbridge Community College where he was a mathematics teacher and now spends his time travelling, playing in the Community Band, acting in Community Theatre, curling, and golfing. This is the second book Lee has worked on with Colin. The first, *The Flavor of Baseball: The First 160 Years* (L. Bean Consulting), was published in 2004.

Part I
Noteworthy Voices

Anthony Henday (circa 1720 – 1780)

Anthony Henday, a fisherman, net-maker, sailor, laborer, explorer, and convicted smuggler, failed in his greatest mission: to persuade Natives of the west to travel to Hudson Bay for the busi-

Henday watches a buffalo hunt. Illustration by Robert Banks, *Canada Then and Now*

ness of trading. However, he did succeed in making Alberta and the west better known to the Hudson's Bay Company (HBC).

Henday, born in Britain, on the Isle of Wight, joined the HBC in 1750. He was "the proper Person sent [a] great way up into the Country with presents to the Indians [and] . . . drawing many Natives to trade" with the HBC rather than with the rival French traders. (*Behold the Shining Mountains!*).

On June 26, 1754, Henday left York Factory on the Hudson Bay and headed for the west with returning Indian traders. They travelled almost 2 000 miles to the Foothills of the Rockies.

After leaving their canoes on the Saskatchewan (Paskoya) River they struck out on foot across the great prairies. Henday had his own "bed-fellow," the term he used to describe the Cree woman who served as his interpreter, cook, and personal companion. He highly valued the advice given by his Cree guide, Conawapa.

After arriving at his destination, Henday could not persuade the Aboriginals to make the long trading trip to the Hudson Bay area. It was, in their opinion, a dangerous and unprofitable trade route. Henday and the Crees wintered in Alberta and built canoes for the return trip. Travelling down the river, they were met by other tribes. Some traded with the Crees and others joined up with the group. When they came to the French forts along the way, Henday was impressed at how well the French traders did in trading with the Indians. By June of the next year, Henday and his fellows were back in York Factory.

Due to poor health, Henday made only short excursions over the next few years. In June 1759, he returned to Archithinue (Blackfoot) Country, but again he failed to convince the Natives to trade with "his" company. One year later, he and 61 canoes of Indians (guides and companions) reappeared at York Factory. He returned to England in 1762.

His family believed that he had served the HBC well but had received little recognition and reward for his remarkable endeavors. It is true, however, that he was one of the first White men to probe the vast west, including the area now known as Alberta. He also advised HBC officials that their trading policies needed refinement and more common sense.

It is interesting that Henday saved £113 of the £120 he was paid during his 12 years of service. He left the HBC heartbroken because he was never promoted above the rank of net minder.

Quotes from Anthony Henday

All quotes taken from Henday's journal can be found in *A Year Inland: The Journal of the Hudson's Bay Company*, unless otherwise stated.

Behold the Shining Mountains!

A comment recorded in Henday's 1754 journal on his sight-ing of the Rockies. He was near present day Innisfail where he met a large camp of Blackfoot or *Archithinues* people who called the Rockies "Mountains of Bright Stones." Henday is considered to be the first European to see these mountains.

I have been sent by the great leader who lives down by the great waters. He invites your young men to come to see him, and to bring their beaver skins and their wolf skins. For the skins he will give them powder, shot guns, cloth, beads, and the like. He will welcome them warmly at our trading posts on Hudson Bay.

This was a supposed Henday comment to an Alberta Indian Chief, Henday encouraging trade with the English traders. The chief's answer disappointed Henday: "It is too far. Our young men do not use canoes; they ride horses . . . the French treat us well." As credited in *Canada: A New Land.*

As I am looked on as a leader, I have ladies of different ranks to attend to me.

Anthony Henday, who added that he had considerable "feast-ing, smoking, drinking, dancing and conjuring" during his 1754 trip through the west.

[T]he friends and neighbouring allies of the Sarcee, the Blackfoot are well supplied with horses.

HBC officials had difficulty believing Henday's report of Indians riding horses. *Fifty Mighty Men,* 1959

October 14. Came to 200 tents of Archithinue (Blackfoot) natives, pitched in two rows, and opening in the middle; where we were conducted to their Leader's tent; which was at one end, large enough to contain fifty persons; where he received us. . . . Our leader set out several grand-pipes, and smoked all around, according to their usual custom; not a word was yet spoken on either side.

October 15. These natives are drest [sic] *much the same as others; but more clean and sprightly. . . . They appear to be under proper discipline and obedient to their leader; who orders a party of horsemen evening and morning to reconnoiter; and proper parties to bring in provisions . . . their clothing is finely painted with red paint; like unto English Ochre; but they do not mark nor paint their bodies.*

October 16. I rode a hunting with twenty men. . . . They are so expert that with one, or two arrows, they will drop a Buffalo. As for me I had sufficient employ to manage my horse. When I came home I was invited to the Leader's tent again. . . . I thought it very curious as there were four different languages amongst us. . . . He gave one of the Leaders two young slaves as a present and 40 buffalo tongues.
Henday's journal for 1754.

Level land, few words and plenty of good water . . .
Henday near Chauvin, September 11, 1754.

I don't very well like it, having nothing to satisfy them on what account I am going up the country and very possibly they may expect me to be a spy.
This was Henday's view that his excursion into the west might make French traders suspicious and angry.

Such remarks I thought exceedingly true.
Henday confirming that Natives travelling to the Hudson Bay region for trade purposes often starved on the journey.

There are scarce a Gun, Kettle, Hatchet, or Knife amongst us, having traded them with the Archithinue Natives.
Henday's comment after his companions (the Cree) traded away most of their goods for furs on the journey back home.

The French talk several [Native] Languages to perfection: they have the advantage of us in every shape; and if they had Brazile tobacco . . . would entirely cut off our trade.
Henday noting the head start and advantage that the French traders had over the "English" HBC traders.

The Buffalo [are] so numerous [we were] obliged to make them sheer out of our way.
> Henday's 1754 comment on what he witnessed on his travel to the Red Deer region.

The water [is] very salt, smells like Brine.
> This journal note suggests that Henday tried to hide his disappointment (and lied?) in finding the Rocky Mountains rather than the Pacific Ocean. Historian Glyndwr Williams, for example, claims that Henday tried to outline his achievements in "a dishonestly optimistic light." in what is now Alberta, Henday was delighted with the *"fineness of the weather, and the pleasant country"* and noted that there were *"plenty of buffalo and the Indians [were] hunting them on horseback."*

Quotes on Anthony Henday

We apprehend Henday is not very expert in making drafts with accuracy or keeping a just reckoning of distance other than by guess.
> Observation made by HBC officials in London who had received reports from Henday re his travels in western Canada. The HBC officials concluded that Anthony Henday was "a bold and good servant." *A Year Inland*

Peter Pond (circa 1739 – 1807)

At age 16, the energetic and shrewd Connecticut-born Peter Pond left home and his father's shoe repair shop to join the army, and served in the Seven Years War. At the end of the war, adventures beckoned and he became a fur trader. In 1775, Pond left the Mississippi fur trade after killing a man in a sunrise duel. He moved north and west to the south Saskatchewan River region. In 1778 he was persuaded to lead a five-canoe probe to take trade goods to the Athabasca region. There the fur trader had a rich harvest. He returned to the area as a partner of the North West Company.

Alexander Mackenzie was Pond's second-in-command during the winter of 1787-88. The 24-year-old Mackenzie was influenced by Pond's often-wrong opinions about the area's geography. The intemperate trader spent months drafting a map showing a mythical North West Passage after hearing from the Copper Indians that the Pacific Ocean was within easy access by rivers linked to Lake Athabasca. (He also observed the tar sands which today are producing great wealth.)

Pond was the first White man to stand where Fort McMurray exists today. Northwest of that area, he grew Alberta's first garden and built "Pond's House," the first structure of its kind in Alberta. In spite of his imaginary route, he did inspire Mackenzie who later became the first white man to reach the Arctic Ocean and the Pacific Ocean.

Pond's reputation for violence lost him the approval and respect of other traders. At the age of 46, he returned to New England and died 19 years later, destitute and largely unknown.

Quotes from Peter Pond

Beaing then sixteen years of age I gave my Parans to understand that I had a strong desire to be a Solge. . . . But thay forbid me, and no wonder as my father had a larg and young famerly I just begun to be of sum youse to him in his affairs. Still the same Inklanation & Sperit that my Ancestors Profest run thero my Vanes. It is well known that from fifth Gineration downward we ware all Waryers Ither by Sea or Land and in Dead so strong was the Propensatey for the arme that I could not with stand its Temtations.

    Caesars of the Wilderness: Company of Adventurers

We met the next morning eairley and discharged pistels in which the pore fellowe was unfortenat.

    Peter Pond on his early morning duel. *Caesars of the Wilderness: Company of Adventurers*

Quotes on Peter Pond

*[. . .] fits right into the tradition of this province, long before any-
one could have predicted the maverick place it would become.*
Observation by Arita van Herk, *Imagine One Big Province.*

*I transmit a Sketch of the North Western parts of this Continent,
communicated by Peter Pond, an Indian Trader from this
province, shewing his discoveries, the track pursued, . . Mr. Pond
proposing some advantage to himself from publisning it hereafter
. . . had requested care may be taken to prevent its getting into
other hands, than those of the King's Ministers. I am told he had
qujitted this province somewhat dissatisfied with the trading
Companyt, whom he served, and with a view of seeking employment in the United States, of which he is a native.*
From a letter by Dorchester in 1790. *Peter Pond, Fur Trader
and Explorer*

*Before them lay a land of wood and lawn and crystal streams, the
pasture of the buffalo and the elk, the gateway to the great park-
lands of the Athabasca, the Mackenzie and the Peace. The
Clearwater carried them swiftly down to the broad Athabasca
above the mouth where they built a post, Old Pond Fort, the first
white settlement in what is now the Province of Alberta.*
This lyrical account by Donalda Dickie refers to Peter Pond
and his men who were attempting to prevent Natives from
trading with the HBC. The canny Connecticut–born trader
later left the fur trade under a cloud having been implicated in
the murder of two competitors. However, in the Athabasca
region the high-strung Peter Pond discovered the richest "fur
kingdom" in North America, yet he died impoverished in
New England. *The Great Adventure, 1965*

Peter Fidler (1769-1822)

Here was a mapmaker, surveyor, explorer, and fur trader
obscured by the remarkable exploits of his contemporary, David

Thompson. In northeast Saskatchewan, Peter Fidler and Thompson had studied under the same Cumberland House instructor, Philip Turnor, who explored and mapped large areas of western Canada.

Born in Bolsover, Derbyshire, Fidler was to have a significant impact on Alberta and the rest of western Canada. He joined the HBC in London as a laborer and was sent to York Factory in Manitoba. Because of his talents, he became a writer and then was sent to Cumberland house to learn surveying. Thompson, who was to have accompanied Turnor on a surveying trip, suffered a broken leg, so Turnor took the young Fidler instead. Their mission was to prove that a river draining into the Hudson Bay could reach the Athabasca area. That fact would mean the area was part of the original HBC grant. However, the Methy Portage ruled out that hope.

Fidler became a qualified surveyor with Turnor's help. He spent a full season in a Chipewyan Camp on the Slave River. (In his lengthy journal, Fidler claimed it was there that he learned to dream in Chipewyan.) In 1802, he led his own party into the Athabasca area where he established the trading post, Nottingham House. There, Fidler, his party, and his Swampy Cree wife, Mary, lived for the next few winters. At his fort, the industrious Fidler studied French, traded furs, argued and debated with the opposition Nor' Westers[1], and operated a bindery and a small hand press.

Peter Fidler was the chief surveyor for the HBC from 1796 to 1822. He explored large areas of the west and prepared at least 32 invaluable maps of the area. The cartographer surely helped to open up the west. He located accurately the Red Deer, Highwood, Battle and Bow Rivers, and he pinpointed the Rocky Mountains.

After his retirement at age 51, he became a supernumerary clerk in the Swan River area of western Manitoba. His health was not good. Some accounts refer to his paralytic affliction and a lack of industry. He was proud of his 14 children (11 survived him) and pleased with the journals and maps that, he stated, would go to the HBC to which he was always loyal.

---

[1]A Nor'Wester, a shortened version North-Wester, was a trader, a servant or wintering partner of the North West Company.

Some experts claim that Fidler was the first European to find coal on the Canadian prairies and may have been the first to record the Chinook winds which exist in Southern Alberta. He was the first trader in Northern Alberta, the second White man to grow a garden there, and the first to be accused of murder. The details surrounding the accusation remain uncertain to this day.

Quotes from Peter Fidler

The following quotes are taken from Peter Fidler's journal published in *Journals of Samuel Hearne and Philip Turnor* unless otherwise stated.

We are so very few—they so numerous!
    Peter Fidler's journal complaint that the Nor' Westers had a distinct trading advantage over their HBC rivals.

English brandy freezes at -26° F, rum at -23° F, Holland gin at -17° F
    Peter Fidler's 1802 observation.

[The Piegans led me to] a creek a little above a high steep face of rocks on the East Bank of the Creek, which the Indians use as the purpose of a Buffalo Pound, by driving whole heards [sic] before them and breaking their legs, necks, & in the fall, which is perpendicular about twenty feet.
    Fidler's journal where he describes a buffalo jump near Rosebud Creek, Alberta.

[It is] called by these Indians "Nin nase tok que" or the King, & by the southern Indians the Governor of the Mountain, being the highest known place they know off [sic].
    Fidler's journal where he describes his sighting of Chief Mountain in Montana from a valley between the Livingstone Range and the Porcupine Hills.

[I got a bearing on] a remarkable High Cliff of the Rocky Mountains called . . . by the Muddy River Indians "Omock cow wat che mooks as sin" or the Swans bill.

Fidler's journal for November 1792, wherein he describes today's Devil's Head mountain near the eastern end of Lake Minnewanka.

I struck Mr. Black with a stick two or three times—Ogden immediately drew his dagger and cut two large holes in the side and back of my coat and pricked my body . . . Mr. Black then took up part of the stick I had broken over him and stuck me on the thumb close at the upper end of the nail and smashed it to pieces . . . Mr. Black and Ogden yet followed me into my room with their guns and dagger and abused me very much while my thumb was dripping.

Fidler's journal. He tells of his fight with opponent traders at Ile-à-la-Crosse near the Athabasca gateway

David Thompson (1770 - 1857)

Of Welsh descent, David Thompson, a short, pug-nosed explorer, trader, astronomer, and mapmaker was one of the greatest geographers who ever lived. He was also a gifted storyteller, a writer whose records and accounts added much knowledge to Canadian history.

David Thompson in the Athabasca Pass, 1810.
Pen and ink drawing by C.W. Jefferys.

Thompson was fatherless at age two. Later his mother placed him in a charity institution called Grey Coat School, near Westminster Abbey, London, where he became an avid reader. The 14-year-old Anglican youth joined the Hudson's Bay Company and soon sailed for Churchill.

Not long after, the youth was sent inland to serve at a post on the South Saskatchewan River. There, while hauling wood just before Christmas 1788, Thompson fell and severely fractured his leg. His year-long recuperation at Cumberland House was filled with surveying lessons from the remarkable Philip Turner, the HBC's resident surveyor. Though he recovered and enjoyed a successful career, Thompson limped for the rest of his life.

An insatiable appetite for travel, navigation, map-making, and exploration replaced Thompson's interest in fur trading. In the spring of 1797, he walked the 75 miles to a post on the Reindeer River where he offered his services to the North West Company (NWC), the HBC's main rival. He knew that his former employer wanted him to focus on fur trading, not map-making. The NWC needed a surveyor to mark the boundary line between Canada and the United States, from Lake Superior to the Lake of the Woods region. Thompson was more than able to complete the task. Later, the NWC sent him to southern British Columbia to explore the Columbia River to its mouth on the Pacific Ocean.

For years the astronomer/mapmaker toiled on the mapping of the huge fur trading territories east of the Rocky Mountains. His comprehensive view of western Canada was the first accurate attempt to map the region. He surveyed 1 900 000 square miles of wilderness during his 28-year stint in the west; in all, he travelled 55 000 miles. The multi-talented Thompson accomplished much in spite of his permanent limp and the increasing loss of sight in his right eye – a result of countless examinations and measurements of the sun through his instruments.

The surveyor spent the winter of 1787/88 on the Bow River not far from today's Calgary. There he learned much from Soukamappe, a Cree who taught him Indian history, customs, and skills. Thompson recorded the stories Soukamappe revealed, immortalizing the Plains Indian history before the coming of White men. David Thompson revered the Indians and their culture, and had a strange mystical streak himself. He revered beavers as near deities, and blamed Europeans for troubles on the frontier. He spoke four Aboriginal tongues and compiled Indian language dictionaries. Natives called him *Koo-Koo-Sint*, the man who looks at stars.

It was to Rocky Mountain House that Thompson often returned from his long journeys. At age 28, he met and fell in love with a bright 14-year-old Métis girl named Charlotte Small. They had a tribal marriage, and a year later their first baby, Fanny, was born at that fort. Twelve other babies were to follow. Their story is one of Canada's finest love stories, one that lasted 60 years. Thompson, who didn't swear, drink, or smoke, remained loyal to Charlotte.

In 1812, Thompson returned to eastern Canada with his wife and family, who were financially settled at the time. Charlotte and David exchanged formal wedding vows on October 30th of that year. Three years later they moved to the Williamstown area of Ontario where David found work as a surveyor. Despite their former abundance, Thompson's generosity to others eventually left the family in a tough financial situation. By 1846 the bankrupt, nearly blind Thompson was weakened by ill health. Two months before his 87th birthday he died, and three years later, the love of his life, Charlotte, died and was buried beside David in Montreal's Mount Royal cemetery. They died in poverty and obscurity.

If J.B. Tyrell had not stumbled upon Thompson's notes and maps it is likely that Canada's greatest land geographer would not be fully recognized today. In 1924, Tyrell found Thompson's unmarked grave. He also found the surveyor's 39 dusty journals, 11 books of field notes, and a huge map of the western half of North America between the 45th and 60th parallels.

Quotes from David Thompson

Quotes taken from David Thompson's journal can be found in *Travels in Western North America*, by Victor Hopwood, unless otherwise stated.

While wintering . . . I fell, breaking my leg, which by the mercy of God turned out to be the best thing . . . when Philip Turner . . . taught me the science of surveying: how to determine longitude and latitude exactly for each post of trade.

David Thompson reflecting on the start of his career.

Such was the competitive nature of these men that they never walked, but always raced over the rough, steep ground at a trot . . .[and] singing as loud as they could.
> Thompson on his voyageurs most of whom were short, weighing around 150 pounds, and often carrying 270 pounds on their backs.

At last the Rocky Mountains came in sight like shining white clouds in the horizon.
> David Thompson's Journal.

Strange to say here is a strong belief that the haunt of the mammoth (Sasquatch) is about this defile.
> David Thompson's Journal.

When advised to be cautious in the hunting of the bison . . . they would laugh and say they killed an ox with the stroke of an axe, and should do the same to the Bisons.
> David Thompson on the Iroquois near Fort Augustus (Edmonton), circa 1798. Thompson claimed the tribe looked down on other First Nations and all Whites.

In the spring of 1799, I came to Isle à la Crosse and there met Charlotte Small, a lovely Métis girl.
> Thompson on the love of his life.

It is my wish to give all my children an equal and good education.
> A letter sent by the cautious and caring father to Alexander Fraser. The surveyor was near Edmonton but added "I hope to see you and a civilized world in the Autumn."

I had made it a law to myself that no alcohol shall pass the mountains.
> David Thompson despised the whiskey-for-fur trade.

Why should such an angelic kind be doomed to be the prey of car-nivorous animals and birds? But the ways of Providence are unknown to us.

Thompson's journal where he comments on the ptarmigan and its sound, *Kabow-kabow-kow-a-e.*

Writers on the Indians always compare them with themselves who are all white men of education. This is not fair. Their noted stoic apathy is more assumed than real . . . but in private he feels and expresses himself sensitive to everything that happens to him or his family.

David Thompson's journal, which clearly indicates that he highly respected the natives, their customs, religions, and ethics.

Thus I have fully completed the survey of this part of North America from sea to sea, and by almost innumerable astronomical observations have determined the positions of the mountains, lakes, and rivers, and other remarkable places on the northern part of this continent, the maps of all of which have been drawn and laid down in geographical position, being now the work of twenty-seven years.

David Thompson's summation of his career in western Canada and beyond.

Quotes on David Thompson

When David came . . . in the spring . . . you cannot know how beautiful it is when the grass is new and soft. He was not very tall but his eyes were dark like ours and his hair dark too, and fine. I liked him from the first day.

Charlotte, speaking of the day that changed her life. She spoke Cree, French, and English. *Woman of the Public Song*

As for this man's achievements they will more than stand the test of time as they are extorordinary.
Woman of the Public Song

I am old now . . . I have seen many winters. Anytime now I must be ready to go to the happy hunting ground . . . [and] hope you will not demand that I pay the debt in the other world.

This story, found in Thompson's journal, tells of an old man's debt to the mapmaker/surveyor. Thompson's response "The debt will be forgotten. Go and make a good hunt in good health."

He was the greatest land geographer who ever lived.

J. B. Tyrell had this message inscribed on Thompson's tombstone.

Daniel Williams Harmon (1778-1843)

A deeply religious man, born in Vermont, Daniel Harmon was distressed over the loose morals he observed furing his 20 odd years in the Canadian West. A clerk for the North West Copmpany, Harmon left the east and travelled to the North West in 1807. He became an expert in bringing better relations between his company and the Indians of the Athabasca District. He was placed in charge of Fort Chipewyan in 1807. In 1811 he assumed the superintendence of the district of New Caledonia and served with distinction until his retirement in 1819.

Unlike many of the traders that had an aboriginal wife, Harmon did not abandon his wife and family when he returned to civilization. He loved Elizabeth Duval and he loved the children born to their partnership. Harmon and his family moved to Vermont where he worked on his journal *Sixteen Years in Indian Country.* In 1843 he moved to Montreal where he died of scarlet fever

Quotes from Daniel Harmon

Some of the principal Indians of the place desired us to allow them to remain at the fort to see our people drink, but as soon as they (our people) began to be intoxicated and quarrel among themselves, the Natives were apprehensive that something unpleasant might befall them also, therefore they hid themselves under beds and elsewhere and said they thought the white people had become mad.

[Later] I invited several of the Sicaany and Carrier Chiefs and most respectable men among them, to come and partake of what we had remaining – and I must acknowledge that I was surprised to see them behave with so much decency and even propriety as they did in drinking off a flagon or two or rum . . .

Harmon's comments on a New Years drinking spree in New Caledonia. *Ceasars of the Wildreness: Company of Adventurers*

Why do you think I have come so far to bring you guns, and powder, and Ball? You know that if you returned with a hundred scalps I would not give you a pint of rum nor a pipeful of tobacco for them; but if you bring back beaver skins you can get anything you want.

Daniel Harmon convincing a war-chief to abandon a scalp-hunting expedition. *Builders of the West*

Thursday, October 10.—This day, a Canadian's daughter, a girl of about fourteen years of age, was offered to me; and after mature consideration, concerning the steps which I ought to take, I have finally concluded to accept her, as it is customary for all gentlemen who remain, for any length of time, in this part of the world, to have a female companion, with whom they can pass their time more socially and agreeably, than to live a lonely life, as they must do, if single.

If we can live in harmony together, my intention now is, to keep her as long as I remain in this uncivilized part of the world; and when I return to my native land, I shall endeavour to place her under the protection of some honest man, with whom she can pass the remainder of her days in this country; much more agreeably than it would be possible for her to do, were she to be taken down into the civilized world, to the manners, customs and language of which, she would be an entire stranger.

Her mother is of the tribe of the Snake Indians, whose country lies along the Rocky Mountain. The girl is said to have a mild disposition and an even temper, which are qualities very necessary to make an agreeable woman, and
an affectionate partner.

To see a house full of drunken Indians, consisting of men, women and children, is a most unpleasant sight; for, in that condition, they often wrangle, pull each other by the hair, and fight. At some time, ten or twelve, of both sexes, may be seen, fighting each other promiscuously, until at last, they all fall on the floor, one upon another, some spilling rum out of a small kettle or dish, which they hold in their hands, while others are throwing up what they have just drunk. To add to this uproar . . . a number of children, some on their mothers' shoulders, and others running about and taking hold of their clothes, are constantly bawling, the older ones, through fear that their parents may be stabbed, or that some other misfortune may befall them, in the fray. These shrieks of the children, form a very unpleasant chorus to the brutal noise kept up by their drunken parents, who are engaged in the squabble.

Daniel Harmon, speaking of some Chipewyan natives, circa 1807.

On the evening of the 15th inst. my woman was delivered of two living boys. They appear, however, to have been prematurely born; and from the first, little hope was entertained that they would long survive.

Daniel Williams Harmon, Feb. 25, 1810.

How could I spend my days in the civilized world, and leave my beloved children in the wilderness? The thought has in it the bitterness of death. How could I tear them from a mother's love and leave her to mourn over their absence . . . ? The [Indian] mother of my children will accompany me . . . [and] I design to make her regularly my wife by a formal marriage.

Daniel William Harmon.

Sir George Simpson (circa 1787 – 1860)

Here is an individual whose talents, exploits, personality, weaknesses, and faults must be shared by most of Canada. As elsewhere in the nation, Alberta was greatly influenced by George Simpson, Governor of the Hudson's Bay Company for four decades. He came to Alberta often.

Sir George Simpson in his later years.
Notman Photographic Archives, McCord Museum of Canadian History

The efficient, if parsimonious, administrator and tireless traveller was "impervious when it suited his purposes and loyal to those whose interests paralled his" (Smith, 1988, p. 2006). After the HBC and the NWC amalgamated in 1821, Simpson began his rule of an empire larger than the one Napoleon had held in Europe. It appears that the Scots-born trader was the right person for such a large undertaking. His goal was to reestablish the HBC monopoly of the fur trade. From the Pacific Ocean to Labrador, the charismatic Simpson displayed his iron will, cost cutting policy, authority, and insistence on profit for the company. In 1841, the young Queen Victoria awarded Simpson with a knighthood.

The world traveller and master politician had at least five children born to his "partners" across Canada.[2] He could be very cruel to his English wife and cousin, Lady Francis Simpson, 26 years his junior. After their marriage it became unfashionable for a White trader to have an Indian wife even though he earlier stated that connubial alliances improved relationships with and protection from natives. Historian Irene Spry commented on Simpson's actions and attitude:

> His sex-object attitude to women was largely responsible for the breakdown of marriage a la facon du pays, which was a humanly decent type of relationship [and] he created a total dislocation in what had been a perfectly valid type of society (Newman 1, p. 261).

---

[2]When he was called "the father of the fur trade," it was often with a chuckle and a wink. Some sources claim he fathered nearly six dozen children across Canada.

From his headquarters in Lachine, Quebec, Simpson ruled his empire until his death leaving his wife and their two sons and three daughters.

Quotes from Sir George Simpson

These quotes are from *Ceasars of the Wilderness, Volume II,* unless otherwise stated.

[Christian teachings appear to be about] filling the pockets and bellies of some hungry missionaries and rearing the Indians in the habits of indolence.
George Simpson in a letter to London.

It has occurred to me, however, that philanthropy is not the exclusive object of our visits to these Northern Regions, but that to it are coupled interested motives, and the Beaver is the grand bone of contention.
Simpson, 1821.

Nine out of ten men are captivated with the phantom, popularity.
Simpson declaring that he wasn't one of them.

I am convinced [Natives] must be ruled with a rod of iron, to bring and to keep them in a proper state of subordination, and the most certain way to effect this is by letting them feel their dependence upon us.
Simpson writing to London in 1822, a year after the HBC and NWC joined. He was describing what kind of governorship he intended to provide to the new HBC.

These chiefs were Blackfoot, Piegans, Sarcees and Blood Indians, all dressed in their grandest clothes and decorated with scalp locks. I paid them a visit giving each of them some tobacco. Instead of receiving their presents with the usual indifference, they thanked me in rotation.
Simpson meeting with chiefs in Edmonton, 1841.

I hope that your horses might always be swift, that the buffalo might instantly abound and that [your] wives might live long and look young.

Governor George Simpson speaking to the assembled Indian Chiefs in Edmonton. *Fifty Mighty Men*

It is strange that all my ailments vanish as soon as I seat myself in a canoe.

George Simpson whose paddlers set distance and speed records on Canadian rivers. Incidentally, Simpson replaced his employees' canoes with the more sturdy York boats where possible. It was considered a high honor, a recognition of courage and stamina, to be a member of Simpson's canoe crew which was expected to handle the 18 foot long canoes for 16 to 18 hours a day.

I do not think that any part of the Hudson's Bay company's territories is well adapted for settlement. The crops are very uncertain.

Sir George Simpson to a committee of Britain's House of Commons in 1857.

In February next, I shall have completed forty years Service with the Hudson's Bay Company. During that very long period I have never been off duty for a week at a time, nor have I ever allowed Family ties and personal convenience to come in competition with the claims I considered the Company to have on me. . . . It is high time, however, I rested from incessant labour. Moreover, I am unwilling to hold an appointment, when I cannot discharge its duties to my own satisfaction. I shall therefore make way for some younger man, who I trust may serve the Company as zealously and conscientiously as I have done.

George Simpson's 1858 farewell letter to the HBC. At the end of his career and busy life he suffered from periods of near blindness. His once imposing frame had shrunk. He missed his wife, Francis, whose delicate health failed after the birth of their second son in 1850.

Quotes on Sir George Simpson

These quotes are from *Ceasars of the Wilderness, Volume II*, unless otherwishe stated.

A bastard by birth and persuasion, George Simpson . . . was one of the few men who lived up to his own Napoleonic pretensions.
Newman correctly claims that Simpson's "style of buccaneering capitalism belong less to an age than to a system."

[The Little Emperor] became a nearly perfect instrument of Company policies . . . preoccupied with the life of the Company with which he fully identified his own.
John Galbraith

The Northwest is beginning to be ruled with an iron hand.
Williard Wentzel, former NWC clerk, on George Simpson's "rule."

No man is more appreciative of downright hard work coupled with intelligence.
Chief Factor John Stuart on how to win George Simpson's approval and promotion.

Simpson must have been one of the best-hated men in North America . . . he existed only as a man of business . . . he is an outstanding example of an immature ego possessed by personal complexes.
Alan Cooke, Montreal Hochelaga Research Institute.

He's na big, but he's built like a Kyloe bull and just as stubborn.
A fellow Scot's comment on George Simpson, the "Little Emperor of Rupert's Land." *Fifty Mighty Men*

[Simpson] was undisputed ruler of one half a continent . . . [and] had been knighted by the Queen.
J. W. Chalmers on the "Little Emperor." *Fur Trade Governor: George Simpson*

George Simpson . . . the real ruler . . . of what is now western Canada, was by no means a wholly admirable character. He was vain and eccentric, intolerant and prejudicial, definitely ruthless, undoubtedly a snob, and notorious for his love affairs. He was also ambitious, courageous, energetic, [and] devoted to his company.

J. W. Chalmers comment on Simpson in *Fur Trade Governor: George Simpson*

One white man was dressed like a woman, in a skirt of funny color. He had whiskers growing from his belt and fancy leggings. He carried a black swan which had many legs with ribbons tied to them. The swan's body he put under his arm upside down, then he put its head in his mouth and bit it. At the same time he pinched its neck with his fingers and squeezed the body under his arm until it made a terrible noise.

This native's account, perhaps apocryphal, tells of the piper honoring Governor Simpson travelling by canoe to Fort Norway. The same piper, Colin Fraser, or a bugler usually welcomed the "birchbark emperor" to Fort Edmonton and other HBC forts in the west. For such occasions he wore his Royal Stuart tartan cloak. The bagpipe's music must have astonished the natives.

Hudson's Bay Factor John Rowand.
Glenbow Archives: NA1747-1

John Rowand (1789 – 1854)

Big Mountain and *Iron Shirt* were names given by Indians to John Rowand, the Edmontonian who also has been called the Czar of the Prairies. He has been recognized as one of the most influential White men on the prairies of 19th century Canada. The short, stocky, fur trader, so highly valued by HBC Governor, George Simpson, earned his reputation for physical courage, fairness, and sound business practices.[3]

The Montreal-born Rowand joined the North West Company at age 14 as an apprentice clerk, posted to Fort Augustus, later called Fort Edmonton. The former rivals, (the HBC and NWC) joined forces in 1820, and soon after, Rowand was named Chief Factor in charge of the Saskatchewan district which included areas around Edmonton, Jasper House, Rocky Mountain House, the Lesser Slave Lake region, Fort Assiniboine, and areas far east of Edmonton. He held that position for nearly 30 years.[4]

Rowand made Fort Edmonton the most important depot for the new HBC and its chain of forts stretching from the Hudson Bay to the Pacific Ocean. The hot-tempered trader used his fists more than his modest education to get the job done. For 50 years he used the Saskatchewan River as a pipeline and highway for the fur trade.

The warm-hearted but bluff trader epitomized early western hospitality. His superior, George Simpson, acknowledged Rowand's "very superior management at Edmonton" which was "the most troublesome post in the Indian country." Profits grew and Rowand became a rather rich man.

In the year of Rowand's birth there were no more than three White men's houses in what is today's Alberta. During his half-century operation from his Edmonton base, John Rowand made a most significant mark on western Canadian history.

It was his temper that killed John Rowand. At Fort Pitt the hot-headed 65-year-old trader rushed to settle a violent fist fight amongst the boatmen. He fell dead.

The family man[5] and trader died and was buried at Fort Pitt even through he had wished to be buried in Montreal. Simpson

[3]Simpson treated Rowand as a friend and confidant rather than as an employee. The Governor took the trader with him for part of his world tour.

[4]It was the custom that a Chief Factor rated 12 buffalo tongues per year. Chief Traders received six tongues.

[5]Rowand's "Big House" in Edmonton boasted the Northwest's first glass windows, shipped from Britain in barrels of molasses.

knew those plans so he had Rowand's body disinterred and had the remains taken to Norway House. As W.E.S. Gladstone reported:

> they got an Indian to dig it up and boil the flash of [sic].It was sayed that the wommen of the fort made soap with the fat of the pot.

Rowand's bones were then taken to York Factory on the Hudson Bay and then by ship to England. Four years after his death the Edmontonian's remains recrossed the Atlantic Ocean, and were buried in Montreal's Mount Royal cemetery.

Quotes from John Rowand

[They] think themselves entitled to be treated and rewarded for having visited us with empty hand as well as if they had filled our stores with beaver skins.
>   John Rowland's angry November 1, 1823 comment about two-dozen Blackfoot who arrived at the fort with only a handful of furs.

They are sullen, timid and desponding under hardship but haughty, vindictive, and overbearing in prosperity and when they have the upper hand over their enemies their cruelties know no bounds.
>   John Rowand on Natives near Rocky Mountain House. *John Rowand: Czar of the Prairies*

We know only two powers—God and the Company.
>   John Rowand, HBC Factor at Fort Edmonton. *Newman (1), pg. 240*

Any man who is not dead within three days is not sick at all.
>   John Rowand. *Newman (1), pg. 240*

The amply gifted Rowand ruled "with something close to inspired tyranny."
>   Peter Newman in *Company of Adventurers. Vol. I.*

Stop, you villains!

Rowand's shout to a body of 200 Blackfoot Indians, "naked and in war paint," who were threatening Rowand's neighbors and him. See Cheadles's Journal, p. 147 for details. The Indians reportedly apologized to Rowand. HBC piper Colin Fraser added that the Indians "actually cried with vexation." *Newman (1), pg. 240*

We put two pigs in a sty to fatten.

John Rowand near Christmas time, 1827. Likely they were among the earliest pigs in Alberta.

He was not big; in fact he was very short, but he was brave, that little man, you know – brave like a lion. He feared no man; not even a whole tribe of Indians could make him afraid.

Father Albert Lacombe on his friend John Rowand.

[There] is a very fine level race-ground, of two miles or more in length; horse racing being one of the chief amusements of the place . . . and here we may observe [it] is not only celebrated for fine women, but for fine horses.

Alexander Ross, associate of Gov. Simpson, on the fine settlement (Edmonton) built by Rowand.

John Palliser (1817 –1887)

In 1847, the 30-year-old Irish hunter, John Palliser, returned home from the American west with a pet wolf-dog and three strong buffalo which mightily impressed the citizens of Comeragh, County Waterford in Ireland. The tall, erect, young man earlier attended Dublin's Trinity College, served as captain in the artillery militia, and as sheriff in his home county.

Captain John Palliser. Glenbow Archives NA-808-1

The straight-backed Palliser caught the attention of Sir Roderick Murchison, president of the Royal Geographical Society, who in 1857 asked Palliser to lead a group of scientists to western Canada to explore, study, and map the plains between the North Saskatchewan River and the Canada-United States border. The society provided £5 000 for that purpose. The British North American Exploring Expedition was also to examine southern passes through the Rockies for a possible railroad route.

When the expedition reached today's Alberta, Palliser was forced to split his group into smaller parties. Thomas Blakiston, astronomer and magnetic observer, travelled south to the Waterton Lakes region before crossing the Kootenay Pass and South Kootenay Pass. Surgeon and geologist James Hector followed the Bow River and travelled through the Kicking Horse and Vermillion Passes. His group also explored the Athabasca River region, the North Saskatchewan River Valley, and Howse Pass. The British zoologists, botanists, geographers, climatologists, and geologists were kept extremely busy under Palliser's leadership.

Palliser seldom raised his voice, which somehow carried well to his listeners all the same. The clarity of his speech and its clear pronunciation drew the attention of his men. His character and sense of decency aroused loyalty and respect among his fellow travellers.

Part of his responsibility was to examine the country's coal and forest resources, and the area's suitability for farming. Another assignment was to ascertain whether one or more practicable passes existed over the Rocky Mountains within British Territory.

The 1857 to 1860 Palliser Expedition produced the first maps of Alberta's mountain regions. He was wrong about the agricultural potential of the prairies, which he termed "an extension of the Great American Desert" and which came to be known as the Palliser Triangle. However, he was optimistic about the fertile park belt, a region extending from the Lake of the Woods to the Rocky Mountains, surrounding the Palliser Triangle.[6]

[6]Palliser's name today honors a triangle of land (area south from Red Deer to the US border and angling southeast to southwestern Saskatchewan),, a hotel, a mountain, a school district, and a political constituency.

John Palliser returned home, made his report to parliament, received many honors, and published maps from his travels. In 1869, the intrepid voyager went hunting in Novaya Zemlya, Russia. He loved to play the music of Bach, and he enjoyed his many walks in the beautiful Irish Comeragh Mountains. After one such walk, the bachelor Palliser collapsed and died. Ninety years later, the Province of Alberta unveiled a plaque in his honor. Sadly in 1923, a fire damaged Comeragh House and destroyed most of Palliser's records and notes.

Quotes from John Palliser

Whenever we struck out on the broad prairie we generally found the soil worthless except here and there.
>Palliser on the prairies of western Canada. *Fifty Mighty Men*

A perfect oasis in the desert we have traveled.
>Palliser on the Cypress Hills after travelling from the Bow River area.

[It] can never be expected to become occupied by settlers . . . although there are fertile spots throughout its extent it can never be of much advantage to us as a possession.
>Palliser's comment on the prairies in Western Canada.

[My associates are] Gentlemen, Scotch-half breeds, American, Canadians and one coloured man, Dan Williams.
>*Fifty Mighty Men*

[The Canadian prairies] are characteristic of the great American desert.
>*Fifty Mighty Men*

These tribes [Blackfoot, Blood, Peigan] are considered by all who know them as the wildest and most dangerous of the aborigines in British territory.

The whole region as far as the eye could reach was at times covered by buffalo in herds varying from hundreds to thousands. The grass was eaten off the earth as if the place had been devastated by locusts.

John Palliser, 1858. *Fifty Mighty Men*

It is great fun to see the black looks of the hostile divines (clergymen), I understand that sometimes hostilities have proceeded further than mere looks.

Palliser's pungent comment on the rivalry among missionaries from different churches.

Almost everywhere along the course of the North Saskatchewan are to be found eligible situations for agricultural settlement; a sufficiency of good soil is everywhere to be found.

John Palliser on the park belt in Alberta.

"Twelve Foot" Davis (1820 – 1900)

"Twelve Foot" Davis on his way to Edmonton. *Glenbow Archives NA-4035-119*

Henry Fuller Davis, prospector and trader, was a unique character in Alberta's history. The illiterate Vermont-born Davis went to the Caribou gold fields in British Columbia where he found a 12-foot strip of unclaimed land between two incorrectly filed claims. The nickname evolved from his small claim and stuck. His rich find allowed him to open a chain of trading sites in the Peace River region where he became known as an honest but shrewd free trader. Because of his physical strength, local Indians called him "the wolf." The crusty, bearded, tobacco-chewing trader became locally famous for his hospitality, and his unwillingness to take a bath. No one was ever denied entry to his shack (and his grub) even when he was absent.

Towards the end of his life the colorful Davis, suffering from increasing blindness and terrible arthritis, would frequently yell to God to "take me up." Walking became impossible, so often his friends would cart Davis in a wheelbarrow.

The life of "Twelve Foot" Davis cries for a moviemaker. He is buried on a hill overlooking the confluence of the Smoky and Peace Rivers. A 12-foot wooden statue graces a park in the town of Peace River.

Quotes from Twelve Foot Davis

Was Johnny Split-toe your father? The answer was *yes.*
Before your father died [10 years earlier] he left some beaver skins with me. I'll pay you now.
"Twelve Foot" Davis, the honest trader, to a native who came by the trader's place of business. Davis, of course, kept no records or books, but relied on his excellent memory. *Fifty Mighty Men*

It was that darned two set me wrong.
Davis reflecting on a mistake: The illiterate Davis in 1892 in his Hudson Hope post received a note asking for his help. The only thing Davis could identify was the number "2" on the page so he sent two bottles of whiskey to the "sick" person who wasn't sick. The note was an invitation to dinner. *A Narrative History of Fort Dunvegan*

No miss, why should I be afraid to die? I never killed nobody, and I always kept open house for all travelers all muy life. No miss, I ain't afraid to die.
"Twelve Foot" Davis to an Anglican sister at Buffalo Bay on Lesser Slave Lake. *Fifty Mighty Men*

I dunno; maybe it's 'cause them fellers all needs smiles and they all needs grub an' I keeps a good stock of both. And so, I just smiles at 'em and feeds 'em.

"Twelve-foot" Davis explaining why he had so many friends.
Fifty Mighty Men

Twelve Foot Davis
Pathfinder, Pioneer, Miner and Trader
He was Every Man's Friend and Never Locked his Cabin Door

Marker on the Grave Site of Henry Fuller Davis

James Carnegie, Earl of Southesk (1827-1905)

Sir James Carnegie, a well-connected Scot and rather rich widower believed that a great adventure and a successful hunt would be just the thing for his health. But where to go? At a friend's home he mentioned his

desire to travel in some part of the world where good sport could be met with among the larger animal, and where . . . I might recoup my health by an open-air life in a healthy climate.
Saskatchewan and the Rocky Mountains

Earl of Southesk. Glenbow *Archives NA-1355-2*

A friend suggested that "the Hudson's Bay country" would suit Carnegie well because "the country is full of large game, such as buffalo, bears and deer [and] the climate exactly what you require." His 1859 "adventure" led to his later book called *Saskatchewan and the Rocky Mountains* (1875).

In April 1859, Carnegie, whose health had deteriorated following the death of his wife, left Scotland, and in April 1859 sailed from Liverpool to New York. He then journeyed to St. Paul, Minnesota and crossed the Canadian Prairies – hunting all the way. His account tells of his experiences in northeastern USA: the Niagara area, Kingston, Detroit, Chicago, and St. Paul among other centres. In Manitoba and Saskatchewan he kept his pen busy. He followed the Macleod River up to the Medicine Tent River area which he claimed had never previously been seen by a White man. The Earl and his crew worked their way to the Kootenay Plains of the Saskatchewan River valley.

In August, he reached Fort Edmonton, and in September, he left the fort and travelled up the Athabasca River. Just one month earlier James Hector of the Palliser Expedition had travelled through the Pipestone Pass and missed meeting with Carnegie's crew. A close miss!

The man took himself seriously. He noted that during his Alberta travels he had "no companion of my own class," and that he should set himself apart from "other mortals." Often during their travels the workers gathered around their fire while the Earl of Southesk found himself alone by his fire. The aristocrat travelled with an India rubber bath thought suitable for the well-bred Victorian traveller. Southesk's troops carried an assortment of guns, each to serve his love of the hunt and trophies, such trophies being the heads of the animals.

Carnegie seemed willing to try anything "strange and exotic." Once, a member of his party killed a skunk and brought it to camp. A visitor wrote:

> I afterwards saw it roasting . . . looking awfully hideous, robbed of it skin and ears, and shorn of the bushy tail . . . [and] I had a hind leg of the skunk for breakfast . . . but there was a suspicion of skunkiness about it that prevented me from finishing the plateful. (*From Saskatchewan and the Rocky Mountains*)

After leaving the Jasper House area Carnegie and his party returned by horseback to Fort Edmonton. He enjoyed the sights, sounds, and experiences he found in the frontier. The hunting and fishing were great, and his companions, Native and European, were delightful. He journeyed back east and then home to Britain.

The earl's book, *Saskatchewan and the Rocky Mountains*, was reprinted years later. Edmonton historian L.G. Thomas noted that,

> [Carnegie] had irritated some of his readers, perhaps because he seems to lack seriousness of purpose that North Americans regard as the only possible justification for the expenditure of the large sum of money Southesk's expedition must have involved.

The earl re-married and had eight children by his second wife.

Although today's readers might consider Carnegie an insufferable snob, he was a keen observer and recorder of his adventures. Southesk Lake, Southesk Pass, Mount Southesk, and Southesk Cairn Mountain were named in his honor.

Quotes from James Carnegie

All quotes are from *From Saskatchewan and the Rocky Mountains*

[Fort Edmonton has] wine, well-made coffee, vegetables, cream tarts and other good things too many to mention.

August 11th – It was yet early when we found ourselves looking down on the broad stream of the Saskatchewan river, from the summit of a high steep bank directly opposite Fort Edmonton, My men advanced and saluted the Fort with a general volley from their guns and rifles, – a summons promptly answered by the dispatch of a boat, which in a short while ferried us across to the northern shore. As we landed, Mr. Brazeau, the officer temporarily in charge, and the Rev. Mr. Woolsey, the Wesleyan missionary of the district politely came forward to meet us and offer their friendly welcomes on our arrival . . . upstream the view was exceedingly beautiful.

The Indians listen to them, pretend to believe and obey, and obtain baptism, but as soon as the missionary takes his leave they relapse into their former practices. All with whom I have conversed agree in thinking that little or nothing can be done to improve the adults of the Cree, Ojibway, Assiniboine, or Blackfoot tribes, and believe the only hope lies in the teaching and influencing the young, before evil and reckless habits become a part of their nature.

In all Indian music that I have heard there is a remarkable likeness to the howling of wolves, mingled with droning growl of a bear. The Blackfeet, however, are said not only to excel all other tribes in music but to have really fine voices.

From Carnegie's diary.

One gleam of consolation enlivened the weary day – an unexpected, far-distant view of two grand peaks of the Rocky Mountains. Over which a thundercloud cast a solemn, leaden shade. It was but an imperfect view, but so marvelous was the contrast between the damn confined darkness of our track through the dripping fir trees, and the sudden freedom of an open sky bounded only by magnificent mountain-forms, that for a moment I was quite overwhelmed.

The changes of temperature are very sudden in these elevated valleys. At noon we were hiding from the burning sun in any shade that could be found, in the evening we were trembling in the icy wind of a premature winter: – but there are no mosquitoes, so welcome cold, heat, wind, rain, fog, anything, if only those tormentors are cut off!

With the buffalo it is the same – kill, kill, kill. All the year round the Indians are hunting and slaughtering them, and in the winter they drive them into 'pounds' by hundreds at a time, and murder every beast in the enclosures, male and female, young and old, usable or useless. Such waste will soon bring its bitter punishment.

For myself – I wore a now only tolerably clean cream coloured hunting shirt of buffalo skin, fringed on the arms and shoulders, grey trousers fasted under the knee with pieces of green braid: and a thin, white, wide brimmed Yankee hat, with the bell-shaped crown pressed in.

I entered an area no European had ever seen, where bears and wild sheep were certain to be abundant.
Commenting on his trip from the Macleod River to the Medicine Tent River area after leaving Fort Edmonton, September, 1859.

John Macoun[7] (1831 – 1920)

John Macoun was born in Ireland and as a youngster, developed a passion for Ireland's outdoors. He became a rather pompous young man as he considered himself morally superior to others because of his virtues. The Ulsterman strongly supported the British crown and the Orange Order.

In 1850, the Macoun family moved to Canada where the young man tried teaching and later served as a volunteer during the 1866 Fenian troubles. He developed a serious interest in the local flora and earned a Master's Degree at Syracuse University. He was to amass a collection of Canadian fauna and flora which became the foundation of the National Museum of Natural Science. The tireless Macoun, "the professor" as he was popularly called, provided agricultural justification for the CPR's southern route. Later, the outspoken plant geographer was named Dominion botanist, and he established the Dominion Herbarium of over 100 000 species. He discovered over 1 000 of them. In 1882, he was named a charter member of the Royal Society of Canada.

The distinguished explorer and naturalist with his heavy white eyebrows, moustache, and beard, was widely recognized in scientific circles. He was proud when his son, John William (1869-1933) became the first Dominion Horticulturist.

Ernest Thompson Seton, world-renowned naturalist, said Macoun was, "the pioneer naturalist of Canada." He pushed back the frontiers of our natural history and clearly added tremendous

[7]Macoun, Saskatchewan is named in his honor.

knowledge to Canadiana. Macoun is remembered as a champion of the agricultural potential of western Canada including Alberta, of course.

Quotes from John Macoun

Long after the noises ceased, I lay and thought of the not far-distant future when other sounds than those would wake up the forest; when the white man would be busy, with his ready instrument steam, raising the untold wealth which lies buried beneath the surface and converting the present desolation into a bustling mart of trade.

> Macoun on the Oil Sands, from his Journal written on a rainy September night in 1875 as he lay under an overturned York Boat. The botanist spent the day inspecting the bitumen beds on the riverbanks near Fort McMurray. Frank Dabbs, *Calgary Herald*

Two miles before we reached the fort we stopped on top of the last slope and looked down over the scene. At our feet lay the Bow River and its beautiful
valley.

Calgary itself lay hidden among the distant trees, quietly nestling under a bluff of light colored sandstone, while about a mile beyond in a little grove could be seen the Catholic mission.

Outside the river valley the prairie extended roll over roll to the horizon, dotted here and there with clumps of bushes, but altogether without trees except in the valleys of the small streams.

Beyond rose the Rocky Mountains like a wall, bounding the horizon to the west and giving a vastness to the picture, which the beholder could feel but not describe.

Walter Butler Cheadle[8] (1835-1910)

Walter Butler Cheadle, centre; and Lord Milton in a headband.
Alberta the Pioneer Years

Walter Butler Cheadle was tall, heavily built, and a physically strong man. It was a glorious morning in 1863 when he and another young adventurer found themselves in the valley of the North Thompson River. The two Englishmen, Cheadle and William Fitzwilliam (Viscount Milton), were thoroughly enjoying the scenery. They were accompanied by an ever changing crew. Cheadle wrote:

> Milton chose a fine hill to the left as his mountain, and I was still higher to the right. His [was] cone-like and terraced, mine [was] a long range of very rugged rocks, very high and snow-clad with green slopes and bright pines half way up. Very fine indeed. (*The North West Passage by Land. or Journal of a Trip Across Canada*).

Mount Milton and Mount Cheadle were named.

If the scenery favorably impressed the pair, their wellbeing caused them greater concern. Through the Rocky Mountain's Yellowhead Pass they travelled, stumbling and starving, to Kamloops. They repaired their condition, visited the famous gold mines of the Cariboo, and made their way to the ship at Victoria, which took them back to England. (Their expedition through Canada's Rocky Mountains surely helped Sir Sandford Fleming's

---

[8] Cheadle, a town east of Calgary, is named in Walter Cheadle's honor.

later successful attempt to find a route for the Canadian Pacific Railway.)

Cheadle described the trip in his 1865 *The North-West Passage by Land* (which ran to at least ten editions), and in his *Journal of a Trip Across Canada*. The trip and his writing had interrupted the studies of the Lancashire-born and Cambridge-educated Walter B. Cheadle, clever son of James Cheadle, Vicar of Bingley, Yorkshire. So Walter returned to Cambridge to complete his medical studies.

In 1884, Cheadle returned to Canada with the British Medical Association, and during his stay he contracted dysentery which permanently affected his health. However, upon his return to England he continued his consultant work, lecturing, writing, and working as an examiner in medicine.

Dr. Cheadle married twice. In 1866, he married Anne Murgatroyd by whom he had four sons. In 1892, he married Emily Mansel, an inspector of nurses. The distinguished physician and explorer earned his reputation for excellence. He has been called "The first Transcanadian tourist."

Quotes from Walter Butler Cheadle

All Cheadle quotes are from his 1862-1863 journal, published later.

Sunday, April 26th.—2 Blackfeet came in, the advanced guard of 6 coming to trade at the Fort; have heard that we have some liquor. Tell them a little for our own use, &c. Better looking & better dressed than the Crees. The men in handsome robes, & dress of blanket, better shaped heads & finer features than the Crees. The women attired in different manner from Cree women, of Chippewas, with long gowns of beautifully dressed buffalo hide, very soft, & dyed brown, with belts round the waist, of leather almost covered with round plates of brass, the size of half a crown. Faces of both sexes highly painted with vermilion. Men's features highly marked; good high foreheads, cheek bones not so prominent as Crees, nose large, well formed, straight, or a little Roman, mouth large but less blubber-lipped than Crees; beautiful teeth like all other Indians.

Thursday, May 14th.—The men took an awful time washing & dressing themselves in their best in order to make a swell appearance at the Fort [Edmonton]. Crossed 4 small streams during the day; water low now & easily forded. After dinner passed freemen on way to Red River, wanted to exchange a mare & foal or lame gelding for Sharman; no go. Arrived in sight of Fort & ahead of the carts, 3 or 4 hours before sundown. Fort very prettily situated on high cliff above the river, banks well wooded. Both of us much taken with the appearance of the place. Descend the hill to the beach, & soon 2 men come across with canoe full of holes & take us over in the barge, which goes back for carts arriving in meantime. Hospitably received by Hardisty. Go down to see luggage landed & find men very screwed [drunk]; been at my rum. Hardisty informs us that there is to be a grand bear hunt at the Lake St. Albans settlement of freeman & Romish Mission, 9 miles from here; that is from Edmonton I believe; 5 bears attacked a band of horses; 2 men narrowly escaped on horseback, one only by throwing his coat to Old Grisly [sic]. Resolve to start at daybreak & join the hunt & get out revolvers & clean guns accordingly.

Thursday, May 21st.—Cantered back to Fort in time for dinner, having promised to send a present to our entertainers. Called at the priest's; gone to river gold seeking. Good looking nun flirting with Norwegian miner who had turned Romanist last winter to obtain a young girl of the settlement.

Sunday June 7th.—In his [Colin Fraser] experience of 38 years in this country never knew an Englishman injured by them. Several Americans killed. Had spent a summer hunting with the Piegans & was treated like a prince. Once when [Fraser was] out with Mr. Rowand, as they were resting in the middle of the day. A body of 200 Blackfeet, naked & in war paint, moved on to them with fearful yells. Mr. Rowand jumped up & cried out 'stop you villains'; one of the chiefs fortunately recognized him & stopped the rest. They were profuse in their apologies & regrets for having fright-

ened them; many of them actually cried with vexation; they had taken them for Yankees, & would certainly have scalped them if they had not recognized Mr. Rowand;

> This June 7, 1863 account repeats the story told by Colin Fraser to Cheadle. The event, some 25 years earlier, involved a hunting trip where the "game was so plentiful they never missed a meal of moose and bighorns." Rowand was HBC Chief Factor at Fort Edmonton.

Thursday June 25th.—All morning along the banks of the Athabaska now more swollen than before. It is fine 1/8 mile broad & full to the banks. On a little bare knoll in the thick wood of the high bank I stopped & awaited the others behind, & had my first view of the Rocky Mountains. A beautiful prospect, & bluish haze softened off the picture very completely. In the foreground below us rolled the rapid Athabaska between its high banks, clothed with pine, spruce & poplar. Beyond, ranges of hills clothed with pines, & running nearly north & south. Farther still & parallel dimly in the haze stood out the first chain of the mountains 'de facto', backed by still higher ones behind; the sun shone on the snow still lying in the hollows & on the peaks. A cleft in the range, cut clean as if with a knife, shewed us what we supposed to be the position of Jasper House & the opening of the gorge through which we were to pass across.

Wednesday July 1st.—Some parts of the [Athabasca] valley were like a garden with wild flowers, the most showy being the Ballardia picta, white & purple vetches, & a brilliant red flower something like the scarlet lychnis in effect. The Fort is merely a little house, surrounded with low paling, very clean looking & pretty, on the west side the river, the ground around covered with wild flowers.

> Cheadle and his crew then entered what is known as British Columbia.

[I]t must be confessed that the Romish priests far excel their Protestant brethren in missionary enterprise and influence.

Cheadle wrote this near Edmonton; he was accompanied by William Fitzwilliam, [Viscount Milton]. Some call the pair the Laurel and Hardy of frontier explorers as they seemed to stumble from one mistake to the next. They once nearly strangled their guide thinking he was an invading Sioux.

[The Catholic Priests] have taught with considerable success the elements of civilization as well as religion [to Indians].

The establishment at Edmonton is the most important one in the Saskatchewan district. . . . It boasts of a windmill, a blacksmith's forge, and carpenter's shop . . . wheat grows luxuriantly, and potatoes and other roots flourish . . . there are about thirty families living in the fort.

Soon after our arrival Mr. Hardisty informed us that five grisly [sic] bears had attacked a band of horses . . . [and then] pursued two men who were on horseback, one of whom . . . narrowly escaped by the strategem of throwing down his coat and cap, which the bear stopped to tear in pieces.

[To enjoy] hunting the buffalo and grizzly bear in the neighbourhood of the rocky Mountains—a glorious life in the far west.
Cheadle and Milton's stated goal.

William Francis Butler (1838-1910)

William Butler, military man, author, and traveller/adventurer, born at Ballyslateen, Ireland, made his mark in western Canada. The ambitious and imaginative man rose to the rank of Lieutenant General.

Butler's first big challenge came when he was assigned by the British government to serve as

Sir William Butler. *Glebow Archives NA-1676*

intelligence officer to the Red River expedition, which was led by colonel Garnet Wolseley. This expedition was to put down the first rebellion or resistance led by Louis Riel. Butler preceded the force to Manitoba and then made his report to Wolseley at Fort Francis.

Commissioned to report on all conditions in the Saskatchewan River country, Butler made his incredible 4 000-mile trip to Fort Carlton and Rocky Mountain House using dogsled, horseback, and by walking. He submitted his report, which is now a gem of western Canadian history. His journey and report provided material for the remarkable *The Great Lone Land*, an 1872 book which is perhaps Canada's finest travel literature as well as a superb historical account. Other books followed including *The Wild North Land* (1873).

In Butler's report he advocated the establishment of a well-equipped force of men to police the west. The NWMP were soon formed because of Butler's advice and other reports and events.

A keen judge of events and people, this passionate individualist and humanitarian was a many-sided personality. It seems that Butler was able to accept the various Aboriginal tribes for what they were, and not view them as noble savages or bloodthirsty villains. However, Butler left Canada to see military service in the Sudan, Egypt, and South Africa. Queen Victoria knighted him. He died at Bansha Castle, Ireland.

Quotes from William Francis Butler

Unless otherwise stated, all quotes are from *The Great Lone Land*.

[Rocky] Mountain house is perhaps the most singular specimen of an Indian trading post . . . every precaution known to the traders has been put in force to prevent the possibility of attack . . . with bars and bolts and places to fire down at the Indians.
Butler observing the named fort.

But to recount the deeds of blood enacted around the wooden wall of Edmonton would be to fill a volume [and] . . . there are many conflicts between these fierce and implacable enemies.

On the Cree-Blackfoot rivalry. *The Great Lone Land.*

It is a curious contrast to find in this distant and strange land men of culture and high mental excellence devoting their lives to the task of civilizing the wild Indians of the forest and the prairie.

Speaking of the Oblate missionaries at Grand Lac (St. Albert), *The Great Lone Land.*

The region is without law, order, or security of property; robbery and murder have for years gone unchecked.

Letter to Lt. Gov. Laird.

Close by to the south lay the country of the great Blackfoot nation-that wild, restless tribe whose name has been a terror to other tribes and to trader and trapper for many and many a year.

Captain Butler made this comment while travelling from Edmonton to Rocky Mountain House, *The Great Lone Land.*

War . . . is the sole toil and thought of the red man's life. He has three great causes of fight: to steal a horse, take a scalp, or get a wife.

William F. Butler after visiting Edmonton and Rocky Mountain House, *The Great Lone Land.*

[There was] a mighty barrier rising midst an immense land, standing sentinel over the plains and prairies of America, over the measureless solitudes of "This Great Lone Lane." Here, at last, lay the Rocky Mountains.

Upon sighting Alberta's mountains, *The Great Lone Land.*

Along the lofty shores of the Peace River the Saskootum berry grows in vast quantities . . . and the bears come forth to enjoy it . . . on such foor Druin grows fat and unwieldy . . . thus falling an easy prey to his hunter.

William F. Butler on the black and grizzly bears, *The Wild North Land.*

*Dogs in the territories of the North-west have but one function –
to haul. Pointer, setter, lurcher, foxhound, greyhound, Indian mon-
grel, miserable cur, or beautiful Esquimaux, all alike are destined
to pull a sled of some kind or other during the months of snow and
ice: all are destined to howl under the driver's lash; to tug wildly
at the moose-skin collar; to drag until they can drag no more, and
then to die.*

Butler after leaving Fort Edmonton.

*[Buffalo] flee from the sight, the sound, and the smell of the white
man. Why does he take the land from us? Who sent him here? He
puts up sticks, and he calls the land his land . . . who gave him the
ground, and the water, and the trees?*

An Indian chief's words, recorded by Butler in *The Great
Lone Land*.

Plains Cree	11 500
Assiniboines	1 000
Blackfoot	6 000
Bloods	2 800
Piegans	4 000
Sarcees	1 000
Total	**26 300**

In 1870, this was the Aboriginal population between the Rocky Mountains and the Red River, as reported by Butler to Lt. Gov. Archibald of the NWT's. The numbers were likely low because Butler did not visit areas which became southern Saskatchewan and Alberta.

Jerry Potts (circa 1838 – 1896)

Jerry Potts was a devoted boozer, gifted linguist, diplomat, brave warrior, and a memorable character who greatly influenced the history of early Alberta. The taciturn, bowlegged, short, sinewy NWMP scout and guide, Jerry Potts or *Ky-yo-kosi* (Bear Child), was a tough frontiersman and an excellent shot.

Jerry was born in Montana, the son of *Namo-pisi* or Crooked Back, a Blackfoot, and Andrew R. Potts, a Scotland born trader. Jerry's father was murdered while he was very young and he was given to an American fur trader who treated him cruelly. The trader, Alexander Harvey, deserted Potts and another trader

Jerry Potts. *Sir Alexander Galt Museum and Archives*

adopted the boy, teaching him to read and write. When he was 12 years old, Jerry moved to Alberta to live with his mother's family. He learned several native languages, the fur trade, the country, and the art of tracking. He also fought alongside the Blackfoot during the battle against the Crees – near Fort Whoop-Up, the notorious whisky fort near today's Lethbridge. He returned briefly to Fort Benton, Montana where he met NWMP offices James F. Macleod, who asked Potts to serve as guide to the force. His 22-year career with the NWMP had begun. Potts helped to persuade the Blackfoot not to join Gabriel Dumont and Louis Riel in the 1885 rebellion/resistance.

The remarkable Potts was a solitary man for the most part. In his last years, the heavy drinker lived with his extended family on the Piegan reserve. He died a respected, gifted man who earned the gratitude of the Force [NWMP] and the natives.

Quotes from Jerry Potts

People are people. It doesn't matter whether they are mixed white and Sarcee, Sarcee and Siksika or Blood and Chinese. All they want is a chance to live a good life with every person keeping from the past whatever he wants.
   Jerry Potts

Dey damn glad you're here.
   Potts's interpretation of the comments made by visiting Indian Chiefs to James Macleod of the NWMP. *Jerry Potts: Plainsman*

Nudder damn hill.

His response to a wary NWMP officer who asked, "what's after the next hill?" during the famous 1874 70-day march west. *Jerry Potts: Plainsman*

No. Stone's lost.

Jerry Potts's response to Colonel Macleod when the officer suggested Potts was lost because he couldn't find the land-mark. *Fifty Mighty Men*

You could shoot with your eyes shut and kill a Cree.

Describing his role in the October 24, 1870 battle between the Blackfoot and the 800 Cree-Assiniboine attackers. The battle (near today's Lethbridge) was the last major Indian war north of Mexico. *Lethbridge News,* April 30, 1890

Sure, a big bottle of whiskey and George Star. I haven't had my moustache trimmed in years.

An older Potts's response when asked if he needed anything. He and Star as young men reportedly fired their revolvers at each other from 25 paces or so and thereby trimming their moustaches. The fellow who missed bought the evening's whiskey. *Jerry Potts*

You white people are crazy. You got plenty of open prairie all around and yet you use a good cup like this to pee in.

To James Macleod who refused to drink water from a cham-ber pot. *Jerry Potts*

Colonel, I guess you leave dem ol' buffalo bull alone after dis, hey?

To James Macleod after the officer and his horse were lunged at by a huge bull. *Jerry Potts*

Quotes on Jerry Potts

Jerry Potts was one of the last and greatest frontiersmen of Canada's Wild West.

From Bruce Sealy, author of *Jerry Potts*.

Thus Jerry Potts is justly called the best guide in the country, for I do not believe there is another one who could have guided us through the [snow] storm as he did.
From the diary of Sergeant W.D. Antrobus, February 12, 1875.

He won the confidence of all ranks the first day out.
NWMP Sam Steele.

He was the man who trained the best scouts in the force, and, in the earlier days when the prairie was a trackless waste, there were very few trips or expeditions of importance that were not guided by him or the men he had taught the craft of the plains. As a scout and guide I have never met his equal. . . . Potts' influence with the Blackfoot tribes was such that his presence on many occasions prevented bloodshed. . . . It would take a large volume to describe even a small part of the usefulness of this man.
NWMP Sam Steele. *The Law Marches West*

Jerry Potts was a Piegan half-breed, and on good terms with all the Blackfoot tribes. A better man for his duties could not have been selected. He did excellent service all the years he remained with the police, which was until his death in 1899 at Fort Macleod, the point at which he had guided us in the fall of 1874.
Quoted in *The Law Marches West*.

Got just the man for you! Savviest little bugger you'd ever want. Speaks all the Indian languages and he can track a four-day-old passing-of-wind. None too clean, of course but he's your man.
I. G. Baler's effusive comment to Major James F. Macleod of the NWMP.

Jerry had a wonderful sense of location. No matter how fierce the storm or how difficult the trail, he led straight and true to the point aimed at, and was never known to be at fault. As a half-breed Piegan Indian he had great influence with the Blackfeet tribes, and many a time trouble was averted solely by his influence. As an

interpreter also he ranked high. Indians are often rambling in their speech in council, saying much that has no bearing on the question at issue. Potts would get to the gist of the matter in a few short terse sentences.
Quoted in *The Law Marches West.*

Many of the chiefs having long names when literally interpreted had them shortened by Jerry. Crowfoot, whose full name was Crow-big-foot, through Jerry came to be known by the abbreviated title. Eagle Tail, the Piegan chief, was originally named Many Eagle Tail Feathers. Many places in Alberta also took their names from his interpretation of them from Blackfoot into English; as High River, the Blackfoot for which was Spitze, meaning Tall or High Timber, Blackfoot Crossing, Sheep Creek, the Old Man's River, 'the river the Old Man played on' and many others owe their names to Jerry Potts' free translation of them from the original Blackfoot.
Quoted in *The Law Marches West.*

Jerry Potts is dead, but his name lives and will live. His memory will long be green in the hearts of those who know him best, and 'faithful and true' is the character he leaves behind him – the best monument of a valuable life.

It was the rare fortune that . . . [the NWMP] found Jerry Potts, who as a modern Moses was to lead them . . . to the end of their difficulties.

Through the whole of the North West, in many parts of eastern Canada and in England, this announcement [of Potts' death] will excite sorrow.
Macleod Gazette, July 17, 1896.

The funeral took place on Wednesday evening and was with military honours. The funeral cortege left the residence of the deceased about 7:30 pm and proceeded to the Roman Catholic church, where the funeral service was said, after which the procession resumed its way to the cemetery, where the body was laid to rest and the customary three volleys fired over the grave the general salute being blown after each volley.

. . .

When one considers the background of Jerry Potts, his upbringing, his schooling, his lack of father's guidance, and his being shuffled here and there, at a time when the frontier was rough and rugged, it makes one appreciate the many accomplishments of this hero – and hero he most certainly was! Any one of his deeds should, and would, make him a noted figure in any land, and his deeds were so numerous it is difficult to account for them all.

Yes Jerry, we hope, up there in your Happy Hunting Ground, that you are riding again with your many good and loyal friends. Maybe you don't consider all the things you did as being great but we do. Canada and the world salute you! May your horses be fresh, and your powder stay dry.

Jerry Potts

On the western plains during the 1870s and 1880s the name Jerry Potts became legendary. The son of Scottish and Blood Indian parents, his skills as a tracker, guide, fighter and buffalo hunter were without peer. In 1874 he came to the aid of the NWMP as a guide and interpreter. For the next 22 years, until his death in 1896, his services and conduct received respect and admiration from all who knew him.

Alberta "Stop of Interest" sign.

John George "Kootenai" Brown (1839 – 1916)

The Irish-born John George Brown was an outstanding character. From such a man are legends born. He was a soldier in India, a scholar, a trader on the Mississippi, a gambler, a scout for General Custer, a prisoner of Sitting Bull, a gold miner in British Columbia, a buffalo hunter and wolfer in Alberta, Indian fighter, and the father of "Waterton National Park."

The bearded, buckskinned, hot-tempered Brown was a quick trigger sort of man. He murdered a man in Montana. At Fort

Benton he had quarrelled with Louis Ell and shot him dead. Brown was tried and acquitted.

John George "Kootenai" Brown. *Sir Alexander Galt Museum and Archives.*

In 1865, he travelled through the Rockies to Waterton (Kootenay) Lakes from which his nickname was derived. Later, he guided the Rocky Mountain Rangers during the 1885 Riel rebellion or resistance.

It was the Waterton area that captured the heart of "Kootenai" Brown. The scholar and visionary campaigned vigorously to make the area a national park. He served there as a fishing officer, then as a forest ranger, and later as park ranger. The small man with the white handlebar moustache became a legend in his own lifetime. He was more than a conservationist and political activist: he bridged the Alberta frontier to the 20th Century.

Two years after Waterton Lakes National Park was named, Kootenai Brown died and was buried there between his two wives.

Quotes from John George Kootenai Brown

Quotes are from *Kootenai Brown: His Life and Times,* unless otherwise noted.

This will be my home.
Brown after his first sighting of Waterton Lakes. *Fifty Mighty Men*

I'll give you five horses for her.
> Brown's 'purchase' from a Cree father of his daughter *Chee-Pay-Qua-Ka-Soon* (Flash of Blue Lightning) who became Brown's second wife whom he called *Neech-e-mouse* (Loved one). Later, Father Lacombe legally married them. *Fifty Mighty Men*

I assumed that it [Saskatchewan River] must flow into the Atlantic or Hudson Bay and that it would eventually bring us to the fringe of civilization.
> Brown, before he joined whiskey traders and wolfers coming from USA to today's Alberta.

It was at this time I received an arrow in the back, close to my kidneys. It was a miracle I was not killed – I thought my time had come – but I pulled it out, an arrowhead two and a half inches long and the head out of sight. The jagged edges caught the flesh as I pulled it out, and it gave me great pain. I had a bottle of turpentine and, opening up the wound, one of my companions inserted the neck of the bottle and when I bent over about half a pint ran into opening made by the arrowhead. This was all the doctoring I ever got and in a few days I was well again.

We all thought our time had come. The Indians had no firearms, but they were all young bucks, 32 of them, no old men or war women . . . they had lots of arrows and they let them fly.
> On his experience fighting Blackfoot warriors in Alberta.

I had settled long before that when the time for squatting came I would come back to this spot.

This is what I have seen in my dreams, this is the country for me.
> Brown on the Waterton region.

Some taught the Flatheads and Kootenais to play poker and this became their great pastime when they visited the store. It took a card shark to beat them . . . I was a foot racer and a good shot, and in competition on the track or with the rifle I could always beat them.

On his experience in his Waterton store and nearby spots.

The old instinct to ride after buffalo again came over me, and I have to admit I always have a keen appetite for any kind of good strong drink.
Near the end of his career as a mountain man.

Describing "Kootenai" Brown

That squaw man whose cabin is full of the works of Shakespeare and Tennyson.

That Oxford man whose vocabulary would fairly wither the grass when he's mad.

That hunter and scholar fellow down by the lake.

That short-tempered fellow who was there before the mountains grew up.

Quotes on John George   Kootenai   Brown

[He is remembered as] a clean fighter, a straight shot, loyal to his friends, respected by his enemies, ready to face any danger, hardship or deprivation without a murmur, and to defend the region . . . from the ruthless attach of poacher and vandal.
B.V. Silversides, *Waiting for the Light.*

Part II
Words from Notable Groups

Aboriginal[9] Voices.

Quotes From and About the First Albertans

[T]he men of the (Snakes) band, leaving their guns, arrived and were placed in the inner circle around the council fire. The Assiniboines, however, concealed their guns under their blankets and at a pre-arranged signal drew them and shot down in cold blood every man of their ancient enemies. They then rushed to the Snake camp and wiped out the rest of the band, with the exception of three young women whom they brought as prisoners to Fort Assiniboine. Here they were stripped, bound and placed in a tent, to be tortured and finally dispatched at a great scalp dance to be held the next day.

W. B. Cameron's account of a bloody incident close to Jasper House, 1840.

On arriving at the tent we found it was occupied by a very hospitable Blood Indian . . . [who] received us with the greatest kindness. Never shall I forget it. We were hungry and they fed us. Strangers and they took us in.

A grateful Robert Rundle speaking of his experience near the Elbow River, 1841.

Heard particulars respecting the poor old Assiniboine woman who was left in the woods to die . . . three men were sent in search of her; they found her . . . dead and partly eaten by birds. Her hair was also gone, supposed to have been taken by the Blackfoot Indians. Such is heathenism.

---

[9]While Aboriginal or First Nations are titles we use now, during the time period covered in this book, "Indian" was the term used for Canada's first people and is therefore used extensively in these quotes.

61

Rundle's journal April 17, 1843.

Some provision should be made for the poor uncivilized being to [whom] by night the soil belongs.

Thomas Blakiston on the plight of Indians, 1859. Blakiston and his leader, John Palliser often disagreed.

We rode up over a ridge while on the plain below the battle was raging. As we rode down the hill slope, I began to sing my war song. I carried a shield in my hand and this song that I sung belonged to that shield. One of the medicine men dreamed that whoever held this shield would not be hit by bullets. While singing, I put in the word, "My body will be lying on the plains." When I reached the line of battle I did not stop but rode right in among the Crees and they were shooting at me from behind and in front. When I rode back the same way, the men made a break for the coulees. As soon as the men got into the coulees they dug a pit. I was lying about 10 yards away on the side of the hill. I was singing while lying there. I could not hear for the roar of the guns, and could not see for the smoke.

The recollection of the 22-year-old Peigan fighter, Mountain Chief, who took part in the famous and last major Indian battle (near today's Lethbridge, Alberta) in North America, 1870.

This march had all the appearance of a retreat . . . It was well for us that the Indians did not prove hostile. None of us would have returned.

A NWMP officer referring to his group which, were lost on their way to Fort Whoop-Up.

Being now in a part of the country [near the source of the Old Man River] open to hostile attack from Bands of lawless Indians we all lay down with our arms loaded for altho' the Blackfeet and Kootanies are friendly to the English we may be mistaken for Yankees.

Robertson-Ross Journal, September 29, 1872, quoted in *Alberta Historical Review*, Summer 1961.

The white men are here to stay. We must accept them. We do not have to be like them, even though they try to make us like them. We can live in peace with them without becoming part of them.

Bearspaw, Chief of the Stony Indians, 1877.

Young men who were known to be quite stout and hearty fellows some months ago were quite emaciated and so weak they could hardly work; the old people and widows . . . [made] many a pitiable tale.

Lt. Gov. Edgar Dewdney at Blackfoot Crossing, 1877, when some natives were reduced to eating their dogs, gophers, and mice.

We want none of the Queen's presents. When we set a fox-trap we scatter pieces of meat all round, but when the fox gets into the trap we knock him on the head. We want no bait. Let your chiefs come like men and talk to us.

Big Bear speaking to the Rev. John McDougall who was delegated to begin negotiations preparatory to the signing of Treaty Number Seven, 1877. Note: Chief Weasel Calf died at age 86 in 1927 at Gleichen. He was the last of the natives who signed the treaty.

We have had enough war. I think we can live without it. If civilization can tame the buffalo so that they are like cattle, the lesson is one I should not forget.

Chief Red Crow after signing Treaty Number Seven, 1877.

The scene in the camp of the Bloods that night is one I will never forget. The braves held a war dance; all were stripped to the breech clout, and between the war songs they alternately recounted their many deeds of valor, occasionally mentioning my Indian name, Ahmucksi-stomach (big Buffalo Bull).

NWMP Colonel A. G. Irvine, near Medicine Hat en route to see Big Bear whose men, in 1878, had stopped government surveyors from doing their work. Irvine's 26 men were well armed. Irvine won the day (AHR Autumn 1963, p. 10).

I'm from the Big Snake tribe; our people are rattlesnakes. When you die, you'll become one of us.

The message Calf Shirt (circa 1844 – 1901), a Blood Indian, received during a vision during the late 1870s. The man had an uncanny ability to handle dangerous rattlesnakes – he often shoved the snake's head down his throat before Lethbridge and Fort Macleod audiences.

We were received very cordially in the chief's lodge, and it was the largest and most comfortable lodge I had seen. The squaws had a large pot boiling on the fire with buffalo meat, blood, and I don't know what else in it, and after we had shaken hands with every brave in the lodge, the squaws came and handed each of us a cup.

In Hugh Dempsey's, *Waiting for the Light*.

We will tie him up and get even with him [Blood chief Maycasto]. They made a laughing move towards him, but the chief drew his revolver and . . . there were two dead Indians and several more wounded.

In *Waiting for the Light*.

I gave that pretty white woman something (rattlesnake) to wear around her neck, but she nearly jumped out of her nice dress to get away from it.

Calf Shirt who claimed he could talk to the rattlesnakes. "The Snake Man," *Alberta History*.

The Indians surrounding it (Victoria, near Edmonton) are making an attempt to settle on their farms, and live by them, but this they fail to do, and trust to the Government to feed them, and I fear they are only getting into lazy and indolent habits.

Richard Hardisty, circa 1882.

The "tum tum" is kept going every night; and has been all winter; and was all summer, and the whole of the year before that.

Frank Oliver, journalist and politician speaking of the beating of the Indian drum near Edmonton, March 17, 1883.

For God's sake come; there is danger of an attack by the Blackfoot.

An 1885 telegram to NWMP officer Sam Steele from the mayor of Calgary.

Tesqua! Tesqua! (Stop! Stop!)

Chief Big Bear shouting to the young warriors who were shooting their nine victims at the Frog Lake massacre, north-west of Lloydminster.

My heart is on the ground . . . I am dead now to my people. They are hiding in the woods, paralyzed with fear. Cannot this court send them a pardon?

Cree chief Big Bear after the Frog Lake massacre speaking to officials at his Battleford trial He was sentenced to three years in the penitentiary because he could not "be excused" for the actions of some of his followers.

The cook at the post was a Spaniard. He was a surly brute, and carried his revolver strapped to his side . . . he had a young squaw, a mere child, whom he was whipping brutally one day. I tried to make him desist, but he turned on me with a snarl, and a move-ment of his hand towards his belt.

The post, an outpost of Healy and Hamilton of Fort Whoop-Up fame, was south of the Red Deer River, in an area fre-quented by wolfers and whiskey traders. (Ibid, pp. 41-42)

I met and shook hands with Stamix Otokan (NWMP Colonel James F. Macleod) at the Belly River. Since then he has made me many promises and kept them all . . . I trust Stamix Otokan.

Red Crow or *Maycasto* (circa 1820 – 1900), a proud Blood known for his sharp temper, common sense and fine judg-ment.

There is nothing at all idolatrous about this ritual.

James Evans, "the man who taught birch bark how to talk" on the Sun Dance (also known as the Thirst Dance or Rain Dance) held near Fort Edmonton. The clever Evans was the "inventor" of the Cree syllabics – giving them a written language.

James Evans writing on birch bark. *Pen and ink drawing by C.W. Jefferys. National Arvhices of Canada*

One day Earth Woman told her husband Sun, "there are only two of us, and dog is useless. I wish we could have somebody else to live with us." He told her, "No, there will only be the two of us." It started at that point that women will always beat men in an argument, because the man finally said, "Oki, let it be your way."

Time passed and the woman had a baby boy. Sun told her, "Please give him a name." The woman said "no." She said, "If it was a girl I would name her, but since it is a boy you give him a name." He told her, "You are right, I will give him a name. His name will be Napi."

Time went on, and the woman said, "I think it is lonely for our son. He is alone. It is better that there be two of them." Sun said "no." But the woman won again. And again it was a boy. Sun named him creator.

The above story by an old man of the Blood Indians is found in full in *Adolf Hungry Wolf, The Blood People.*

The Indian sent his messages by mirror, fires, smoke and by striking stones together beneath the water, and the same primitive messages were frequently conveyed many miles, and with great clarity, to those who recognized the signals.

Fort Macleod druggist John Higinbotham quoted in Jack Dunn's "Moggasin Telegraph," *AH,* Spring 1997.

In a short thirty-year period [Beaver Indians of northern Alberta] had become so dependent on the white man's traps and guns and

*ammunition that many starved when the traders closed their posts
and thus denied these things to them.*

> J.G. MacGregor, *The Land of Twelve-Foot Davis,* quoted in
> Jacques Hamilton "Explorers," *Our Alberta Heritage.*

*One day a young chief shot his arrow through a dog belonging to
another brave. The brave revenged the death of his dog, and
instantly a hundred bows were drawn. Ere night had fallen some
eighty warriors lay dead around the camp, the pine woods rang
with lamentations of the women, the tribe had lost its bravest men.*

> W.F. Butler's account of the struggle between two factions in
> the Beaver tribe near Lesser Slave Lake.

*No men in this land hunt better than the Beavers. It is not uncom-
mon for a single Indian to render from his winter trappings 200
marten skins, and not less than 20,000 beavers are annually killed
by the tribe on the waters of the Peace River.*

> Captain W. F. Butler near Fort Vermilion.

*We're the People, the worthwhile people. Around us live the less
favoured people.*

> A Beaver Indian, late 19th century.

*There is no doubt that the civilization of the Whitefish Lake band
of Indians is very largely due to the influence of Mr. Steinhauer
who, being of their own race, enjoyed their confidence to a far
greater extent than a white man could possible have.*

> *Edmonton Bulletin* January 17, 1885. Rev. Henry Bird
> Steinhauer, who died in 1884, served other Natives as a cler-
> gyman and leader, for 44 years.

*The Indians found a native drum on the trail and beat it incessant-
ly that night, singing their native ya-ya-ch-ya. Mr Brenlin said no
white man could give the same intonation as the Indians to the
weird ya-ya.*

> Mrs. Robert Holmes, a missionary's wife on the trail to Lesser
> Slave Lake 1902. *Alberta Historical Review,* Spring, 1964.

Crowfoot (Isapo-Muxika) (1830 – 1890)

A tall, lean, dignified man with a chiseled face, the warrior, peacemaker, diplomat, and the "Chief of the Chiefs" was a leader who earned our respect and admiration. Yes, Crowfoot (his full name Crow Big Foot, was likely changed by the Métis scout, Jerry Potts) must be placed on any list of great Albertans.

The Blood Indian, born not far from today's Lethbridge, many times proved his courage in battle. He learned to despise the whiskey traders, recognized the value of the NWMP, helped to keep the Blackfoot and many Crees from joining the 1885 rebellion-resistance led by Louis Riel, and served as negotiator-spokesman at the signing of the 1877 Treaty Number Seven. He died a revered and honored man.

Crowfoot. Glenbow Archives NA-1241-98

The Chief of Chiefs conferred with other leaders of his time: Father Lacombe, Jerry Potts, John McDougall, Colonel James F. Macleod, Red Crow, and officials in Ottawa, among others. He fully realized that the old days were gone forever.

Crowfoot lost most of his children to tuberculosis and smallpox, and pneumonia took the Chief's life. He was buried with his rifle and saddle near Blackfoot Crossing where Treaty Number Seven was signed. At his death, his best horse was shot so that he would have a horse to ride "over there."

Crowfoot Quotes

Our land is more valuable than your money. It will last forever. It will not perish as long as the sun shines and the water flows, through all the years it will give life to men and beast. It was put there by the Great Spirit, and we cannot sell it because it does not belong to us.

We all see that the day is coming when the buffalo will all be killed and we shall have nothing more to live on, and then you will come into our camps and see the poor Blackfeet starving, I know that the heart of the white soldier will be sorry for us, and they will tell the Great Mother, who will not let her children starve. We are getting shut in. The Crees are coming into our country from the north and the white men from the south and east. They are all destroying our means of living, but still, although we plainly see those days coming, we will not join the Sioux against the whites, but will depend upon you to help us.

Though our enemies be as strong as the sun, as numerous as the stars, we will defend our lodges.

You dogs, you have shot Good Heart. You have killed the Man of Prayer.
> Crowfoot's shout to his Cree enemies during a heated battle when Father Lacombe was injured. From Grant MacEwan's *. . . and Mighty Women Too.*

This is the place where the forked tongue is made straight. When my people do wrong, they shall come here.
> Chief Crowfoot after attending a Fort Macleod trial of two Natives charged with various offences. *Fifty Mighty Men*

From Blackfoot Crossing, via Gleichen, N.W.T., 11th April, 1885:

On behalf of myself and people I wish to send through you to the Great Mother the words I have given to the Governor at a Council here, at which all my minor chiefs and young men were present. We are agreed and determined to remain loyal to the Queen. Our young men will go to work on the reserves and will raise all the crops they can, and we hope the Government will help us to sell what we cannot use . . .

Should any Indians come to our reserve and ask us to join them in war we will send them away.

The words I sent by Father Lacombe I again send: We will be loyal to the queen whatever happens. I have a copy of this, and when the trouble is over will have it with pride to show to the Queen's officers: and we leave our future in your hands.

Telegram from Crowfoot to Prime Minister John A. Macdonald.

Father Albert Lacombe
Glenbow Archives NA-19-1

Three years ago when the Mounted Police came to my country, I met and shook hands with Stamix Otokan (Col. Macleod) at the Belly River. Since then he has made me many promises and kept them all – not one of them has been broken. Everything that the Mounted Police have done has been for our good. I trust Stamix Otokan and will leave everything to him.

The white people are as thick as flies in summer time.

Crowfoot after his 1886 train trip to Ottawa with other Chiefs and Father Lacombe. From Grant MacEwan's *Fifty Great Men.*

While I speak, be kind and patient. I have to speak for my people who are numerous and who rely upon me to follow the course which in the future will tend to their good. The plains are large and wide. We are the children of the plains, it is our home and the buffalo has been our food, always. I hope you will look upon the Blackfoot, Bloods, Piegans and Sarcees as your children now and that you will be considerate and charitable to them. They all expect me to speak for them, and I trust the Great Spirit will put into their breasts to be good people, also into the minds of all men, women and children of future generations. The advice given to me and my people has proven good. If the police had not come to this country where would we all be now? Bad men and whiskey were killing us so fast that very few of us would have been alive today. The Mounted Police have protected us as the feathers of the bird protect it from the frosts of winter. I wish all my people good and trust that all our hearts will increase in goodness from this time forward. I am satisfied I will sign the Treaty.

Crowfoot on September 22, 1877.*I hope you will look upon the people of these tribes as your children now and that you will be charitable to them. I wish them [whites] all good and trust their hearts will increase in goodness*

Crowfoot at the 1877 treaty signing at Blackfoot Crossing.

No, I will be the last to sign; I will be the last to break the [1877] Treaty.

I Crowfoot, having lately heard that Poundmaker has been arrested and taken to Regina for having been connected with the rebellion, wish to say that I sent word to him to remain loyal, but my words did not reach him until he had been persuaded into joining the half-breeds. He being my adopted son and we having been together a great deal in past years, I have great affection for him and would request the Great Mother, through the Chiefs in Regina, as a personal favour to me, to grant him pardon, with the understanding that he remains loyal in future and I promise to use my influence to the same end.

Letter from Crowfoot to Governor Dewdeny asking mercy for Poundmaker after the 1885 Rebellion-Resistance, "Death of a Son," *Western Profiles.*

Dear Poundmaker, I send you word that the Agent and other white men say you are well used, and I should like you to send word if it really is true. . . . I have such a feeling of lonesomeness of seeing my children dying every year and if I hear that you are dead, I will have no more use for life. I shake hands with the Agent and Mr. Dewdney, and I know they will do what they can for you. I would like to hear from you direct, how you are treated. Your father, Crowfoot.

Crowfoot's letter to Poundmaker serving time in the penitentiary in Stoney Mountain, Manitoba.

Why should the Blackfoot create trouble? Are they not quiet and peaceable and industrious? The government is doing well for them and treating them kindly, and they are doing well. Why should you kill us, or we kill you? Let our white friends have compassion. I have two hearts – one is like stone, and one is tender. Suppose the soldiers come and, without provocation, try to kill us. I am not a child – I know we shall get redress from the law. If they kill us, my tender heart would feel for my people.

Crowfoot in an 1886 interview with *Toronto Mail* reporter George H. Ham at Blackfoot Crossing after the false rumor that the Bloods were joining with U.S. tribes to make war against the White settlers. "Death of a Son," *Western Profiles.*

Your words make me glad. In the coming of the Big Knives with the firewater and quick shooting guns, we are weak, we want peace. When you tell us about this strong force which will govern with good laws and treat the Indians the same as white men, you make us rejoice. My brother, I believe you and am thankful.

Crowfoot to Rev. John McDougall. *Fifty Great Men.*

Before you [Red Coats] came the Indian crept along; now he is not afraid to walk erect.

A little while and I will be gone from among you, whither I cannot tell you. From nowhere we came, into nowhere we go. What is life? It is a flash of a firefly in the night. It is a breath of a buffalo in the winter time. It is as the little shadow that runs across the grass and loses itself in the sunset.

Crowfoot supposedly said those words just before he died in his tepee overlooking the Bow River in 1890.

Quotes on Crowfoot

The good words of Crowfoot are appreciated by the Big Chief inOttawa. The loyalty of the Blackfoot will never be forgotten. Crowfoot's words shall be sent to the Queen.

Prime Minister John A. Macdonald's telegram read to Crowfoot and the Blackfoot Nation.

I have rarely seen a more touching sight than the poor infirm chief, with his finely chiseled countenance and bright smile leaning heavily on his staff and looking worse than any of his followers . . . contrasted sadly with the Victoria medal which he wore on his breast.

Rev. James MacGregor on the ailing Chief Crowfoot.

The chief had been ill for some time, and on Tuesday last, Dr. George was summoned and found him suffering from pneumonia. The scene in the teepee of the dying Chief was exceedingly impressive, there being about 40 Indians assembled, including the three wives of Crowfoot and Medicine Men from both camps. . . . The day before yesterday, Sapoo Muxima (Crowfoot) went into a swoon and his relatives, believing him dead, killed his best horse before the teepee for his use in the happy Hunting Ground. He, however, revived. When the great Chief breathes his last, his death was taken quietly; he had told the Indians not to mourn and to make no noise. A few days before his death a will was drawn up for him and in this document he left his house and one of his medals to his favourite wife, the rest of his medals and horses to his brother, Three Bulls who is now Chief. The Medicine Men received 15 horses."

Lethbridge News, May 7, 1890.

Men, women and children, mourn over your great parent, you will no more hear his voice and its eloquent harangues. In your distress and misery you will no more rush to his tent for comfort and charities. He is gone. There is no one like him to fill his place.

Funeral oration honoring Crowfoot, given by Father Albert Lacombe.

Swift Runner (circa 1839 –1879)

It took the jury only 20 minutes to decide the fate of Swift Runner (*Kakusikutchin*), murderer and cannibal. The large Cree killed and devoured eight members of his family near Fort Saskatchewan. Earlier, he had been a fine family man, good hunter, and part time worker for the HBC. However, he became a "victim" or follower of the Windigo psychosis, a belief that a man-eating monster lived in the cold northern woods of Canada. Somehow, Swift Runner claimed, the Windigo[10] invaded his body and mind. Thus, the man became a human Windigo with an insatiable hunger for human flesh. "The man had no anchor other than the powerful evil spirit."(Thomson, 2)

Swift Runner. Glenbow Archives NA-504-1

[10]The Windigo psychosis is an aberration characterized by an undeniable, intense compulsion to eat human flesh. Many people today would consider a human Windigo to be insane. (There have been dozens of examples of "Windigo instances" in Canadian history.) Audible and reverberating for miles, the Windigo's blood-curdling hiss and thunder-like roar escape through its jagged teeth and large lipless mouth. Nothing can stop the naked cannibal spirit. Somehow the giant Windigo takes possession of a person's mind, body, and soul, and turns the heart to ice.

The slaughter took place in 1879 and he was arrested on May 27th of that year. On December 20, he was hanged in Fort Saskatchewan. Many Natives, some wearing war paint, and local White settlers attended the execution on that bitterly cold morning. Sheriff Edouard Richard and comrades had ridden from Battleford to supervise the execution.

In any case, a unique relationship developed between the condemned man and Father Hippolyte Leduc. Father Leduc believed he converted the man to Christianity. The priest displayed admirable courage, tenacity, and charity to Swift Runner.

Canadian Natives, as recently as 1950, have declared that they saw the monster in the northern woods. The Windigo legend led to numerous murders across Canada. Family and friends of a victim have killed the human Windigo for the sake of survival (Alberta History, 1979).

Quotes from Swift Runner

Quotes are from *Swift Runner*

At the moment the devil [Windigo] suddenly took possession of my soul . . . I killed the last of my children and ate him.

Whiskey made me feel like a wolf.

Why don't you call me a Cree and not an Indian. You come from tribes, don't you?

This was my wife.
> Statement to police as the cannibal put his fingers into the eyeless sockets of a skull.

I did not kill anybody's children only my own.

Wah wah, you would make fine eating; there must be that much (holding up three fingers) *fat on your ribs.*
> A questionable comment by the cannibal to one of his jailors.

Quotes and Headlines on Swift Runner

SAD CASE OF CANNIBALISM
A WHOLE FAMILY SLAIN AND EATEN
Our Edmonton Correspondent mentions the arrest of a Cree Indian, whose name being translated signifies the Swift Runner, on the horrible charge of having killed and eaten his whole family. Sub-Inspector Gagnon with a party of the police took the prisoner to the scene of the alleged atrocity, and there found the bones of all the family but one. They showed that they had been cooked – some by boiling and others by roasting – thus establishing the charge of cannibalism. . . . The charge brought against him . . . is that he killed his whole family, dried their flesh, and ate it at his leisure.

 Saskatchewan Herald June 30, 1879.

A HORRIBLE TALE!
MURDER AND CANNIBALISM IN THE FAR WEST
Arrest of the Suspected Brute
A most horrible tale comes to us from the Far West – a tale of CANNIBALISM AND MURDER so sickening in its details that we doubt if its equal was ever heard of . . . . They have an Indian in jail here for EATING HIS WIFE AND FOUR [sic] CHILDREN, who died of starvation – at least he said they did; but it is suspected that the redskin MURDERED SOME OF THEM himself. Capt. Gagnon, Dr. Herchmer, and three mounted policemen went out to examine the remains the other day, taking the supposed murderer with them as a guide.
. . .

A DAINTY MEAL
The Doctor had a bag full of bones and four skulls with the flesh all off of them. The doctor said they had been boiled. The bones were broken, and the marrow taken out, and the skulls were also smashed in, and the brains extracted.
. . .

The culprit was taken before the colonel in the afternoon, and was shown one of the skulls. He took it in his hand, and nonchalantly turning it round and round remarked that it was his daughter's and the brute actually smacked his lips!

Manitoba Free Press, July 4, 1879.

The death-warrant of the Indian cannibal confined at Fort Saskatchewan has arrived. When it was read to him he smiled; but it is difficult for any ordinary mortal to see just where the laugh properly came in.
Saskatchewan Herald, December 29, 1879.

.I have seen the power of grace working visibly, sensitively on a hard and savage nature.
Father Leduc after his discussions and prayers with Swift Runner.

He had slept the greater part of the night. I said to him, "Have courage, my son, to the end. Today you will leave this world of suf-ferings, and pains, and privations, and you must endeavor to die as becomes a Christian. Man has condemned, but God has forgiv-en you. In a few minutes you will receive your God for the first and last time in the Holy Communion. He will come to you under the appearance of bread, and in three hours more you will meet him and see him face to face. Have confidence in the mercy of God, and remember what I told you of the good thief [on the cross]."
Father Hippolyte Leduc.

The knot is the secret of it, really.
A hangman's comment at Fort Saskatchewan.

Byes, oh byes, [that's] the puriest hanging I ever saw, an' I've seen thrity wan iv thim.
Jim Reid, an old miner who witnessed the execution.

Well, Jim . . . never before did you see a man and his whole fami-ly, not to mention a brother-in-law and a mother-in-law, drop all together at the end of a single rope.

A police sergeant's response to Jim Reid's comment. (gallows humor?)

HOW THEY GATHERED HIM IN
DETAILS OF "SWIFT RUNNERS" TAKING OFF
A Nervy Cannibal

Fort Edmonton, N.W.T., Dec 23. – The first execution in The Canadian territories took place at Fort Saskatchewan, a mounted police outpost twenty miles from here, on the 20th inst., the victim being Swift Runner. . . . [The area is] infested by Inidan cut-throats and by the refugees who find it to their interest to keep clear of the sheriff and civilization . . . and the efforts of the police to drive or starve them out have never succeeded. Swift Runner's crimes are of the most revolting character

. . .

His contact with white men, however, ruined him. Although whiskey is barred in the territories, very large quantities of it nevertheless find their way in, in bottles disguised as patent medicine, Swift Runner became inordinately fond of it and when half drunk was the terror of the whole region. Six feet and three in height, and of extraordinary strength, he was an ugly customer to meet when on a spree, and the police gave him a wide berth on such occasions. At length his conduct grew so outrageously bad that they sent him back to his tribe, but his old habits clung to him, and he turned the Cree camps into little hells. He said whiskey had demoralized him and made him feel like a wolf.

. . .

The Indians unanimously approved of the sentence. The Indians, who never before saw or heard of death by hanging, were anxious to know if it were a species of torture, and Swift Runner said if it would suit the police he would kill himself with a tomahawk, and save the hangman further trouble.

. .

In the afternoon the Indians held a grand feast, rejoicing at being well rid of a most accomplished villain.

The more intelligent of the Indians living near the scene of the tragedy will feel very much aggrieved if an example is not made of this "bad Indian."

Press report.

*[I]n three days I shall be hung. But I repent sincerely what I have
done . . . I am the least of men [and] do not merit even being called
a man.*
>Father Leduc's quoting Swift Runner. Possibly an edited
>statement.

In the name of God, I will give you the indulgence of the dying.
>Father Leduc to Swift Runner.

I then saw a little below me his poor frame hanging.
>Father Hippolyte Leduc.

*In consideration of the great weight of the prisoner – two hundred
pounds – the drop was made but six feet.*
>Press report.

*The cannibalistic Windigos strike from the north during the first
moons of the winter and will restlessly haunt out lands searching
for food as far to the south as the snow belt extends. Windigos
have been known to attack during the summer but this is very rare.*
>From *Sacred Legends of the Sandy Lake Cree.*

Release them, please.
>Father Lacombe's plea to authorities concerning three natives
>who in 1899 killed another native possessed by Windigo, the
>cannibal spirit. The man had threatened to kill and eat his
>neighbors. The three Lesser Slave Lake men were released:
>their "law" prevailed. For other Windigo-related cases, see
>the book, *Swift Runner.*

Minority Voices

It is a horrible truth that minorities were mistreated and
racism was a way of life. The disproportionate ratio of positive to
negative quotes about and from minorities is mostly an indication
of the powerlessness of the minorities and is not a preference by
the authors or publisher.

Blacks

Black men were part of Alberta's old west, even if they weren't as numerous as their White or Aboriginal contemporaries. For example, around 1818, Grand Michael served the HBC in the Peace River District, as did Crawford Glasco in the Athabasca region, while the hardworking, ambitious John Ware later gained legendary status.

Some of the terms in these quotes, even though not acceptable today, are included here to maintain the integrity of the original quotes.

These unsophisticated savages, however, had their curiosity most strongly excited by a Negro of the name Pierre Bungo. This man they inspected in every possible way, twisting him about and pulling his hair . . . and [concluded that he] was the oddest specimen of a white man that they had ever seen. These Negroes . . . were universal favorites with the fair sex of the red race . . . and [later] we saw many an Indian that appeared to have a dash of the gentlemen in black about him.

Sir George Simpson reflecting on his 1822 visit to Blackfoot country near today's Lethbridge. *Fur Trade Governor*

A real old timer passed on . . . in the person of Dave Mills. . . . Old Dave as he was known came to Alberta during the early days of the early traders. . . . His mother was a blood woman and his father a coloured man. He acted as interpreter during the treaty at Blackfoot Crossing.

Lethbridge Herald, April 11, 1918. Mills was a Black-Indian frontiersman.

The garrison [on the Red Deer River] consisted of six men, which included the manager and interpreter. The interpreter was a Negro. I was told that the Negroes master the Indian language more quickly and easily than the white man.

Donald Graham, 1873. *The Law Marches West.*

Kenedy I hear by
Worne you that Com and Gett your

Personal property if eny you
Have Got of my prmeeis In 24 hours and then
keep
away
from me because I shal Not betrubbled Nor trod
on
only be her most Noble
– Majesty Government (SGD) D. T. Williams

Dan Williams' ultimatum of April 12, 1873, in a note to HBC factor, George Kennedy Williams of the Peace River district. Dan was an ex-slave who believed the Company had built a fort on what he called his land. He recognized only two "authorities": the Queen and his own rifle. Butler's observations on Williams are found in *The Wild North Land*. (On the back of the note Williams added: *"I have waited longe A-Day for an ancer from that Notis you toer-Down and now It is my turn to tore down."*)

His [Dave Mills] conduct . . . has been highly satisfactory and through his knowledge of the Bloods he has been mainly the means of saving the goverment several thousands of dollars.

Agent Cecil Denny, 1884, on the heavy-set interpreter, bull worker, scout, and runner, Dave Mills – a "black red man." Father Lacombe married Mills and a Blood woman, *Poosa* (the Cat). After her death Mills married Holy Rabbit Woman, daughter of a great war chief. *The Law Marches West*

I say, boss, I don' keer to put de court and de sheriff to trouble on my account. Jess lemme off ag'in wid a repriman', as you did las' week, on acxcount ob hit being my fust offense, an'll plead guilty ter five chickens I pulled las' week, on account ob hit being my fust offense, an'll plead guilty ter five chickens I pulled lad' week' and a hog I stole las' winter, an' a pair ob shoes from de store, an' a woodpile I'se gwineter haul off to-night.

Macleod Gazette, October 17, 1884. This so-called "news" item is typical of the racist "humor" of the time.

John Ware (circa 1845 – 1905)

The 230 pound, six-foot ex-slave, cowboy, rancher, and family man surely put his brand on Alberta's history. Born in South Carolina the cowpuncher moved to Texas, then to Montana, and on to Alberta.

Ware disliked sheep, as did many cattlemen, and his rifle focused on the coyotes and wolves – the bane of the sheep men. He was considered by those who knew him to be one of the

John Ware. Glenbow Archives NA-263-1

best horsemen of all times and broke numerous broncos. He also enjoyed steer wrestling and roping.

Ware loved the grass in Alberta and by 1890 he had enough money saved to purchase his own ranch located on Sheep Creek near Millarville. He chose 9999 as his cattle brand because he believed that 9 was his lucky number.

With his Prince Albert coat and spade-shaped beard he was an impressive looking man – especially to the 19-year-old Mildred Lewis, from a strong black family near Calgary. On leap Year Day (February 29, 1892) John and Mildred were married. Their marriage produced five children. A sixth child died in infancy. In 1900 the Wares moved to a Brooks aea homestead. Mildred died of pneumonia five years later in the spring of 1905.

On September 12, 1905, Ware's horse stepped into a badger hole throwing him to the ground. The saddle horn that had known Ware's hands a thousand times found his chest. John Ware died instantly. His favorite dog stayed by his body until help arrived.

John died just 5 days after Alberta became a province. It was forty years since the end of the American Civil War and the end of his being a slave. He had seen the last of the buffalo and perhaps the first automobiles in Alberta. The funeral held in Calgary was the largest up until then.

Ware was well liked and respected for his cheerfulness and honesty. His reputation as a man of courage, strength and skills has given him legendary status.

Metoxy Sex Apee Quin (Bad Black White Man) was the name given to John Ware by some natives.

Quotes from John Ware

Sheep just eat too close to the ground and will spoil the grassland for cattle.
John never liked sheep much. He maintained a cattle ranch.

I'll tell you . . . they're a great lot of boys, an' full of the devil, you bet.
John Ware on other Alberta cowboys. *Macleod Gazette*, 1885.

If you can separate this hoss from me you can have him but don't forget you're starting this show.
John Ware to a would-be horse thief.

Quotes on John Ware

We've decided not to fill that position.
Store manager to John Ware, who applied for an advertised position. It was Ware's first visit to Calgary.

If you want to hire me, you'll have to take my partner too.
Bill Moodie, cowboy, to rancher Tom Lynch (often called King of the Cattle trails). Lynch agreed even after he learned that the partner was the Black John Ware.

Reads: Sheep Creek, Dec 27, 1887

Agreement between Samuel Courtney & John Ware both Ranchers of Sheep Creek. Samuel Courtney agrees to sell all his cattle branded DC on left side and cattle brand inclusive for the sum of twenty seven hundred dollars $2700——.

John Ware to take delivery of cattle as they run on the range. Which sum of $2700 price of cattle is to be paid by John Ware in three year old beef steers at fourty [sic] dollars per head. To be delivered in one bunch on Fall roundup of the year eighteen hundred and eighty eight.

Samuel Courtney agrees to deliver on demand one five year old horse branded IS on right shoulder and DC on left thigh for the sum of one dollar.

Would you believe it, but I'll be dog-garned if those fellers [cowboys] didn't stand on the shore at me, an' me just drownin' all the time . . . them fellers, they just stood and laughed, an' one of 'em says; "get wet, John?"
    John Ware report, *Macleod Gazette,* June 23, 1885

He convinced me that black is a beautiful colour, one that was reserved for God's most cheerful people. The one whose remains we bury today was indeed one of God's gentlemen. His example and message on brotherhood should be entrenched in our hearts.
    The Baptist minister at the 1905 funeral of the cowboy, rancher, and pioneer John Ware.

Yes, he was a man who made the best of whatever a situation might be.

I remember being taken to the woodshed when I was bad. We were made to mind.

He was our dad, a good father, and we loved him.

The above quotes are from an interview with Amanda "Nettie" Ware, John's daughter. She was a prominent citizen of Vulcan, Alberta until her death in 1989.

JOHN WARE KILLED
Well Known Colored Ranger Meets Sudden Death

Brooks, N.W.T. Sept. 12 – John Ware, commonly called "Nigger John", an ex-slave from the south and for twenty five [years] a rancher and cowhand in the west, owner of a thousand head of the finest range cattle on the Red Deer River, was killed today by a horse stumbling and falling upon him, killing him instantly.

Deceased was 60 years old and leaves a family. Ware was one of the most widely known ranchers in the district. He was famous as a roper and rider, and always won first money in any of the competitions he entered. He was a man of prodigious strength, and with apparent ease he could pick up an 18-month-old steer and throw him ready for branding. Any person who has tried to throw a six-months old steer will realize that this feat is no small one.

Ware first came to Canada with Fred Stimson and the Bar U cattle. He was with them for some years, then was foreman of the large Macpherson ranche and later on of the Quorn ranche on Sheep Creek. He started for himself on Sheep creek and ran a ranche there for nine years, removing to the Red Deer, where he has since lived. His wife died this spring.

The Daily Herald, Calgary, September 12, 1905.

Jesse Williams (circa 1841 – 1884)

The often drunk ex-slave from Texas was well known among the 450 citizens of Calgary. The American Civil War veteran, when facing his own execution, noted that he had earlier faced death two times during the American Civil War (1861-65)

On a February night in 1884, the heavily liquored Williams robbed and killed a Scot-born clerk, James Adams, using a razor and an axe. Police quickly captured Williams at an Indian camp some four miles from the town. He was living with a Sarcee woman known as "Religious."

Throughout the trial Williams wore a thirty-pound ball and chain and the six-man jury brought in a guilty verdict after only five minutes of deliberation. Williams, defended by lawyer James Lougheed, was not surprised.

Jesse was correct in at least one respect; many settlers wanted "Judge Lynch" to execute him. In having held Williams in custody, said one letter to the editor, the police force had failed to protect the peaceful town. The anonymous citizen added: "If they do not, they will soon find out that the citizens both can and will ferret out these offenders and punish them in a summary manner." It was noted that there was no shortage of telegraph poles for such a purpose.

On March 29, 1884, the citizens of Calgary – the angry and the curious – gathered to watch Williams's execution. A 16-foot scaffold had been erected on the west side of the fort at the back of the officers' quarters. After saying, "I am here through drink," and vowing that he would meet his victim in heaven, the condemned man walked with a priest to the waiting rope.

The execution of Jessie Williams was the first public execution in Calgary.

Quotes from Jesse Williams

I am here through drink.
Williams comment while on the scaffold.

My crime I know to be horrible, and could any atonement of mind undo the wrong I have done, I would willingly make it. I do not grumble at my sentence.
A statement attributed to Williams.

I was going to ask the judge to give me two six-shooters and hold off the police, and then turn me loose to the citizens of Calgary, as they wanted me so badly. I would have made a short work of some

of them. After I had killed a few of them the rest would have run and I would have made off. At any rate, if they did kill me, it would have been better than waiting here so long.
    Calgary Herald, April 2, 1884.

The executioner then proceeded to adjust the rope around the criminal's neck, after which he drew on the black cap and stood back to see that all was in readiness. At the moment there was a breathless silence, till, seeing everything was complete, the executioner seized an axe, and with one blow severed the rope attached to the bolt. There was a crash and the form of the wretched man disappeared below the scaffold. On going below, it was found that the fall, although about seven feet six inches, had not succeeded in breaking his neck and he struggled convulsively for the space of seven minutes. The body was allowed to remain suspended during an interval of twenty minutes, when life being quite extinct, it was cut down and placed in a coffin.
    Calgary Herald, April 2, 1884.

Chinese

Canada's national railway would never have been completed on time without the help of Chinese workers. Over 16 000 Chinese were employed on the railways. They were assigned the worst and most dangerous tasks while receiving the lowest wages ($1/day) and they did not get the same quality of food and shelter as the White men. The conditions were treacherous and over 700 men died. After the railroad was completed in 1885, they struggled due to poverty and racist treatment, and were unable to be with their families due to the infamous head tax[11] placed on the Chinese by the government.

There weren't many prominent Chinese at this time but one of note would have been Jimmy Smith. In March of 1890 Smith, an elderly oriental Calgarian, died because of inadequate

---

[11]Between 1882 and 1923 Chinese immigrants to Canada paid a head tax. Today there is a demand that the Canadian government make amends for that discriminatory tax.

medical services. He bequeathed $100.00 towards the building of a public hospital in his will. His lawyer, James Lougheed presented the money to the hospital foundation and in November of that same year the Calgary General Hospital opened with 8 beds.

In 1896 a Chinese cook at the Okaloosa Hotel in Canmore climbed a nearby peak on a bet of $50.00 that he couldn't go up and back down the mountain in 10 hours. He started at 7:00 am and returned in time for lunch. No one believed him so the next day he returned with some of the disbelievers and they discovered a flag he had planted there the previous day. For years the mountain was called "Chinaman's Peak." Today it is correctly named Ha Ling Peak in honor of the Chinese immigrant who came to Canada to work on the railway and later became a cook.

[The Chinese] should be made to look up to our ideas of civilization.
   Calgary Herald, August 19, 1892.

The simple fact is that they are one people and we are another. They have one system of life and we have another.
   Calgary Herald, August 19, 1892.

In this way, by consulting the interests of the public safety, we may render the stay of Chinamen in Calgary useless and, in a short time, without any interference with personal liberty, we can be rid of what the majority regard as an obnoxious element.
   Calgary Herald, August 5, 1892. In many articles, Chinese were portrayed as criminals. A Chinese man supposedly brought the 1892 smallpox outbreak to Calgary from Vancouver. By 1900 there were only 60 to 80 Chinese in Calgary.

ATTACK ON CHINESE
A dispute arose between a white man and a Chinaman . . . employees of the Banff Springs hotel. . . . They were in each other's way and the Chinaman said something objectionable to the white man who . . . struck the heathen in the face making his nose bleed and blackening one of his eyes. Within an hour . . . the case was dealt

with by the magistrate who fined the white man $5 and costs. . . .
The magistrate regretted that this record had to be entered in the
books.

From the court's point of view the Chinaman could not be held
responsible for the offence because a man cannot be permitted to
take the law in his own hands for the purpose of resenting an insult
offered by a Chinaman.

Whether or not the heathen was to blame for the breach of peace
it is a reasonable conclusion that had not the dozen or more
Chinamen been imported here the court records would yet be
clean. Chinamen and white men do not mix any better than glue
and perfume.

Banff Cragg and Canyon, May 16, 1903.

The Law and Outlaws

An old trader named Fred Wachter, but nicknamed Dutch Fred,
had begun farming on Belly River [and] he shot and killed his
partner, but as there were no witnesses . . . he was acquitted.
From *The Law Marches West.*

The Police came sixty-two years ago [1874]. The Red Coats (Ma-
Ksi-sik-ka-sim-i) were brave men. They went after the whiskey
traders and they always got their man. I remember one of the first
whiskey traders . . . [named] Money in Blackfoot. He had killed
many Indians. His gun was far superior . . . he was frozen to death
southeast of Cardston.

An elderly Blood Indian named Mike Oka told this account to
his son-in-law Harry Mills, in 1936.

We all hate Estapomau or Money.

A Blood Indian's comment on William Bond, a half-Mexican,
half-Black whiskey trader. The powerful Bond, the first cap-
ture made by the NWMP – and the first to escape the force

was known to have killed men with his fists. He raped native women and cheated other traders in southern Alberta.

Ordinarily speaking, no more widely impossible undertaking was ever staged than the establishment of Canadian authority and Canadian law throughout the western prairies by a handful of mounted police.
> Alberta politician and journalist Frank Oliver some 20 years after the famous 1874 police march to "the great lone land."

If Jarvis had asked us to follow him to the North Pole, not one of us would have refused.
> NWMP officer Jean d'Artique, a former math teacher on the leader of the barnyard troop, Inspector William Jarvis, who left the main group and headed for Edmonton in 1874.

We knew from experience that wherever the English flag floats might is right, but we had no idea that the persons and property of American citizens would be trifled with.
> This angry 1874 report in the Fort Benton Record tells of the alleged mistreatment handed to the Americans who were running business at Fort Whoop-Up. The NWMP were blamed.

I find the Mounted Police delightful. Thanks to them, troubles caused by whiskey traffic have ceased, [and] . . . travellers may cross our plains without fear . . . they do not have . . . to be alarmed about their scalps . . . they truly have given society and the country a fine service.
> Bishop Vital Grandin, circa 1876.

John, you're coming back with me and going to work.
> Cattle king Pat Burns's comment to the horse thief who sold Burns's horse to buy whiskey. Burns had considered calling the NWMP.

I ordered [officer] L'Heureux to open the flap over the entrance of the lodge. Holding my right hand on the butt of my revolver I seized the Métis by the back of his collar with my left hand. I whirled him around through the door . . . [and] I found the lodge surrounded by hundreds of Indians, all of who[m] looked sullen and hostile.

NWMP officer Samuel Benfield Steele arresting an individual in the presence of many Indians including Chief Crowfoot.

One thing they have in this country, and that is law, and it is lived up to. When a man breaks the law here, justice is dealt out to him quicker and in larger chunks than he has been in the habit of receiving in the States, and he gets very little chance of appeal when guilt is fastened upon him beyond a doubt. It is not an old-time western lynch law, but a law made by the Queen, and lived up to and enforced by her people.

Clint Boardman, May 20, 1883, during the track laying area east of Calgary. *Alberta History*, Winter 2001.

Duty became hard and unpleasant, if not unbearable. The men were grumbling so much that the Sgt. Major heard of it and sent the Troop Orderly to the Mess Room at Breakfast time to tell us that if anyone had complaints, to make them at once as he would lay them before Major Crozier without delay. At about half past eight we went to the Sgt. Major, in a body, and made a number of complaints at which he took a full list, promising to see the Commanding Officer and let us know the result as soon as possible.

A reflection of the dissatisfaction among some NWMP members at Fort Macleod, 1883. "Mutiny at Fort Macleod," *Alberta History*, Summer 1995.

You lads are all tenderfeet and have visions before you of taking part in a Neck-tie Social. There never has been a lynching in Canada, nor will there be as long as our force has the police duties to perform, so go away like sensible men and remember that any attempt at lynching will be bad for those who try it.

Sam Steele of the NWMP speaking to an 1884 Calgary lynch mob who threatened to hang Jesse Williams, a black drifter who murdered a young Scot-born clerk, James Adams.

That's Sam Livingstone; let him go.

Leader of desperados to his armed men who had "held up" Livingstone and crew on their way to Fort Macleod from Montana. Earlier Livingstone, while serving on a jury, had voted to let the man go free.

My Grandpa seen 'em often here.
    The statement made by a High River resident regarding the famous pair, Sundance Kid (Harry Longbaugh) and Butch Cassidy (Robert Le Roy Parker). Hollywood made the duo even more famous.

Thoroughly likeable fellow was Harry [the Sundance Kid], a general favorite with everyone, a splendid rider and a top-notch cowhand.
    Fred Ings of the Midway Ranch (circa 1889) who added that "The Kid" feared neither man nor devil. Some suggest that Butch Cassidy visited the cowboy in Calgary. "The Sundance Kid in Alberta," *Alberta History*, Autumn 1994.

All the best criminals go to Paddy Nolan.
    Newsman Bob Edwards on the Irish lawyer (born on March 17) who arrived in Calgary in 1889. The famed after-dinner speaker in jest claimed that "Fort Macleod is an outlying point and the men I know there can out-lie those of any district in the North-West." Nolan defended Cashel[12] and Mother Fulham[13] among many others.

All who wish to look on me once more, look now . . . What I have done, that was bad. But let me tell you that I never thought to lift my hand against a white man . . . I liked to fight. I took many scalps . . . I am not afraid to die.
    Wandering Spirit, a Cree who, with others, was found guilty of the Frog Lake massacre northwest of today's Lloydminster. He plunged his knife into his side but missed his heart. With

[12]Ernest Cashel arrived in Alberta in 1902 and was arrested for forgery, stole a horse, and robbed and killed his employer (a rancher). After an extensive manhunt, he was found dressed in the rancher's clothes. He was convicted of murder and subsequently hanged.
[13]See Mother Fulham quotes on pages 140 and 142.

five other murderers, he was hanged in Battleford and buried in a shallow mass grave. For decades the bones and skulls were exposed. Children and adults fingered the remains. Not until 1954 was cement cover placed over the common grave. A chain link fence was added.

[The masked men] stripped off my drawers, but not my shirt, rolled me on the floor, and put tar and feathers on me from my waist downwards, on my head and face and on my arms and hands.

James Donaldson who was tarred and feathered in Lethbridge in 1895. Apparently after Donaldson "crudely" attended the funeral of Charles Gillies, the gang attacked the man who had had an affair with Gillies's wife. Gillies had taken his Winchester carbine, placed the barrel in his mouth, and pulled the trigger. "Tar and Feathers," *Alberta History*, Spring 1995

Charcoal was tried, found guilty and sentenced to hang. He died like a true warrior, singing his death song all the way to the scaffold.

NWMP officer Sam Steele on the Macleod district's Charcoal. On October 13, 1896, Charcoal shot and killed a Blood Indian, Medicine Pipe Stem. A great manhunt resulted that included 100 police and six-dozen Aboriginals. On November 10, he shot and killed Sgt. William Wilde of the NWMP. After Charcoal was captured, he attempted suicide by slashing his wrists. On February 10, 1897, he was hanged at Fort Macleod. Still weak from his suicide attempt, which was aggravated by his prison hunger strike, he was too weak to stand. He was hanged sitting in a chair.

You [Charcoal] have been found guilty of the charges of killing Medicine Pipe Stem and Sgt. Wilde. You have received a fair trial on both charges . . . there is only one sentence that the law allows me and that sentence is death. I cannot hold out any hope of clemency on the part of the Crown. You must, therefore, prepare to meet your Maker.

Judge Scott's sentence after the jury took eight minutes to render a verdict. Hugh Dempsey in *Charcoal's World*.

I don't want to shoot you, but I'm in a bad position.
Murderer Ernest Cashel who was sentenced to be executed on December 15, 1903. A smuggled gun allowed Cashel to escape from his Calgary cell.

If you do get me it won't be alive. Just tell Mr. Radcliff (the hangman) he mite [sic] as well go back to Ottawa, and take [his] scaffold with him.
Escaped murderer Ernest Cashel's written taunt of defiance to the NWMP. Cashel was recaptured, and on February 2, 1904, he was executed.

James Farquharson Macleod (1836-1894)

Born on the Isle of Skye, Scotland, Macleod was educated in Ontario and practiced law near Bowmanville, Ontario. He served as brigade major with the famous 1870 Wolseley expedition, which met the challenge of Louis Reil's resistance (or rebellion) in Manitoba. There he met the remarkable Mary Drever who later became his wife.

As NWMP Inspector Cecil Denny later reported, there were many other challenges waiting in Western Canada:

Violence was in the saddle
over Canada's west-battle, murder, and sudden death, a composite of evils, which, from the Red River to the Rocky Mountains, year by year exacted a grisly toll.
The Law Marches West

James Macleod had his work cut out for him.

Macleod was the first assistant commissioner of that initial force of NWMP members who were to bring peace to 300 000 square miles of tough country. The whisky trade was to be eradicated, and following the Mounties' Great Trek of 1874, Macleod established his command at Fort Macleod. Earlier the force had been stationed at the famed "whiskey centre" at Fort Whoop-Up.

On the outside, Macleod was calm, competent and self-sufficient. On the inside, he was a vastly different man. He pined for his sweetheart, Mary, fought a constant battle against loneliness and fretted about the men. His was the most difficult job in the force. As assistant commissioner he was the connector between French in command, the officers, and the men. He could not afford to get too close to anyone, but he needed the confidence of everyone.

> Macleod also ended up being policeman, judge and jury for the astonishing multitude of indiscretions the men seemed able to commit. Macleod, being Macleod, didn't complain, though his senior officers were appalled that French treated him little better than a constable. The only person who knew how Macleod felt was Mary. (Cruise and Griffiths, 1997, p. 217)

The Blackfoot confederacy and Macleod soon developed a mutual respect. The Indian leadership respected his reputation for firmness and justice. In tribute, Bull Head, the Peigan chief, bestowed the policeman with his own name, *Stamixotokan*. (Different spellings are used for the Peigan name, meaning "Bulls Head.")

James Macleod is credited as helping negotiate Treaty Number Seven with the Siksika, Pikani, Stoney, Tsuu T'ina, and Kainai people. With many others he signed the 1876 treaty (as did his wife, Mary) in the presence of thousands of people. He had previously signed the 1876 Treaty (Treaty No. 6). Never before had such a large number of natives been assembled on the western plains of Canada. Inspector Denny later reported: "They [the natives] always spoke of the officers of that force, Lieutenant Colonel Macleod, especially, as their benefactor." *The Law Marches West*

Earlier, when it was time to name the fort on the Bow River, James Macleod mentioned an old Scottish castle on the Isle of Mull that once belonged to the Macleod clan. *Calgary*, which in Gallic means clear Running Water, was the name of that castle. The name seemed to describe the Elbow and Bow Rivers: Fort Calgary came into being.

The police officer-judge who gave Calgary its name was buried in that settlement. Today there are some people who suggest that in terms of Treaty Number Seven, his importance has been exaggerated. However, his integrity and intellectual courage cannot be denied.

Quotes from James Macleod

Discipline, a full stomach'll do wonders for discipline.
James F. Macleod to Colonel French.

I'm sorry, sir, I can't allow this to happen. You haven't a shred of real evidence. Even if you did, we've got a lot more serious problems than a few missing biscuits. I can't allow this. I won't allow this.
James F. Macleod to Colonel French who had threatened to put men in irons because of an alleged theft of biscuits. Macleod was worried about the force's morale and French's leadership. French left for the east on September 27, 1874, and the defacto command of the NWMP was transferred to Macleod.

Fancy bumping into you boys.
James Macleod's comment after he rode hard to find some of his missing and lost officers.

They don't look like much but they're good boys. They're good boys. Soft outside but hard inside. They won't run they'll fight.
Macleod speaking to guide Jerry Potts about the mounted policemen on their way to Fort Whoop Up.

So your story is that you own this fort and that it was never used for whiskey trading. Well, let this be fair warning. From this day on, I'm the law out here and I'll arrest anyone I even think is trading whiskey. I've got the authority to try any man and with a wink from Ottawa, I'll hang him.

Macleod to Charles Conrad and Dave Akers of Fort Whoop Up after the NWMP arrived there. The "owners" of the fort had just invited Macleod (who had expected assistance from many whiskey traders) to supper. See these and other Macleod items in the excellent *The Great Adventure* by David Cruise and Alison Griffiths. Denny's book adds further information.

You say that I have always kept my promises. As surely as my past promises have been kept, so surely shall those made up by the Commissioners be carried out in the future. If they were broken I would be ashamed to meet you or look you in the face; but every promise will be solemnly fulfilled as certainly as the sun now shines down upon us from the heavens.

NWMP's Col. James F. Macleod speaking to Indian chiefs at the signing of Treaty Number Seven. From *Red Crow: Warrior Chief.*

Quotes on James Macleod

An escort consisting of one hundred and eight police, one hundred and nineteen horses, and two nine-pounder guns was detailed to accompany Lieutenant Governor of the North-West Blackfeet and other Indians, know as Treat Number Seven. The commissioner, Lieutenant-Colonel Macleod, had previously sent out messengers to warn the Indians of the time and place of the meeting. The treaty was made at the Blackfoot Crossing of the Bow River, about ninety miles from Fort Macleod. It is estimated that the Indians had not less than fifteen thousand horses and ponies with them. His Honor the Lieutenant Governor of the North-West Territories expressed his unqualified satisfaction with all the arrangements that had been made, and the service performed by the police.

The comptroller's report to Ottawa on the signing of Treaty Number Seven.

Cecil E. Denny (1850 – 1928)

Cecil E. Denny
Glenbow Museum NA-1096-1

Cecil Denny (later Sir Cecil Denny) was born in Hampshire, England. In his homeland, as well as in France and Germany, he received his formal education. The adventurous Denny moved to the Chicago area at age 19. In February 1874, he moved to Toronto where he received a commission as Captain in the NWMP. He was one of the original 300 members of the force which he served for eight years.

Denny assisted in the construction of Fort Macleod and in 1875 he was placed in charge of the detachment, which built Fort Calgary. For good reason he was recognized by his superiors as a "young officer of great promise." He knew intimately such figures as Chief Crowfoot, Jerry Potts, James F. Macleod, among others. Among the Indians he was known as Chief Beaver Coat owing to the overcoat he often wore.

After leaving the force in 1882, Denny became Indian Agent for the Cree and Assiniboine Indians and was located at Fort Walshe. His signature is on the 1877 Treaty Number Seven. While later ranching near Fort Macleod, Denny was asked by the Prime Minister to take charge of Western Plains Indians during the 1885 rebellion/resistance led by Louis Riel at Batoche. He helped to keep the local Indians at peace.

Later, Denny served as Police Magistrate at Fort Steele, British Columbia. From 1904 to 1906 he led the NWMP pack train exploring the Peace River area. After that experience he became a Fire Ranger in Northern Alberta. From 1922 to 1927, he was Archivist for the province of Alberta.

Denny died in Edmonton and was buried in the RCMP plot in Calgary's Union Cemetery. He never married. His book, *The Law Marches West*, is a Canadian literary classic.

Quotes from Cecil Denny

The following quotes were taken from Denny s Book, *The Law Marches West.*

These [Métis] hunting parties were annual affairs. They slaughtered thousands of buffalo, as several carcasses were required to make a sack of pemmican weighing about one hundred and fifty pounds. Much of the meat was left rotting on the prairie. A hundred or more animals might be killed in a single hunt and the waste was enormous (p. 29).

We were witnesses of a thrilling scene on this journey – thousands of buffalo swimming the Bow. . . . thousands of buffalo around us were a guarantee against starvation (pp. 36-37).

On the way to the Fort [Whoop-Up] we passed a dead Indian lying by the side of the road. He was an Assiniboine, and had been killed by the Blackfeet. The body had shrivelled like a mummy's in the dry air; he was minus his scalp. (p. 42).

The Blackfoot nation in 1874 numbered eight thousand. Of our civilization they knew nothing. . . . They were extremely fond of tea and drank great quantities. Tobacco they generally mixed with dried red-willow inner bark or the leaf of a small shrub with a red berry, plentiful on the hillsides, called by them ah-so-kin-oky. This leaf gave the tobacco a very aromatic flavour. The women did all work in camp, setting up and striking lodges, cooking, tanning robes, sewing, etc., while the men loafed, ate, and smoked, or boasted of past exploits and planned raids against their enemies (p. 49).

The plains Indians . . . were extremely jealous of their women, much more so than the Crees, and their punishments for infidelity were most cruel. Death was often the penalty, but more frequently mutilation – the nose cut off close to the face (p. 51).

A brighter side of the picture was that the Indians [near Fort Macleod] were most hospitable . . . we were always made welcome (p. 59).

We [NWMP] spent our first Christmas in Alberta in the new fort. . . . buffalo hump was served in place of roast beef, but we had real plum pudding. A dance followed, our partners half-breed girls (p. 59).

The animals covered the prairie in immense numbers. At times one might travel over miles of territory and, as far as the eye could reach, see nothing but buffalo, or ride at an easy lope through countless thousands streaming ahead and behind (pp. 59 – 60).

Ace Samples [near High River] was a noted pistol shot, deriving his nickname, Ace, from his ability at twenty-five yards to hit the ace of any card four times out of five (pp. 61-62).

A tent required ten to thirty skins [of buffalo] for the making. Enormous numbers died from wounds and were eaten by wolves . . . and the large grey prairie species ran in packs. (p. 60).

These whisky traders . . . with few exceptions, were not a bad lot, and many in time became good law-abiding citizens (p. 65).

July 1875 was a month to become memorable in Canadian North-West history . . . for steamer Northcote arrived at Fort Edmonton on her maiden trip, the first boat to navigate the Saskatchewan (p. 77).

[At the HBC store near Morley] They had an assortment of goods which would be curiosity today – flint-lock muskets, Hudson's Bay hooded duffle capots, pigtail tobacco sold by the fathom, carrot tobacco in three-pound rolls, the heavy Hudson's Bay knife which could be used as a hatchet when required, and many other articles now as rare as the dodo, but which had been traded by this company for generations (p. 86).

We found the remains of an Indian and also those of a white man lying near the Elbow River. They had been killed in a drunken fight the previous year (p. 87).

While the buffalo roamed the plains it was useless to let the cattle run; the bulls would attack and kill the domestic steers. (p. 90).

The [Edmonton] fort was heavily stockaded, with bastions at the corners, . . . It comprised a number of buildings, including stores, warehouses, the chief factor's residence, and the officers' quarters. It was well stocked with goods. A few half-breeds lived in cabins, and some Cree Indians in lodges near the Fort. Heavy timber covered the whole country beyond. A number of visitors with dog trains had recently arrived, and the howling of the dogs . . . made sleep impossible for us. (p. 91).

A fair sized horse fast enough to run buffalo would always fetch a good price from the Indians (p. 107).

By 1878, a dozen or more homesteads had been taken up in Alberta. (p. 130).

In 1879 the pay of the [NWMP] force was reduced to fifty cents a day (p. 140).

At the bottom of a gully . . . the searchers came upon the body [of Constable Grayburn of Fort Walshe] with a bullet hole in the back of the head. . . . He [star Child] was tried at Macleod for murder [but] in the absence of any evidence, the jury could do nothing but bring a verdict of acquittal (p. 142).

Grayburn was the first member of the famous force to be murdered while in service.

The town of Edmonton [in 1880] consisted of only five white families and a number of half-breeds, but people were beginning to be attracted there and soon what was known as claim-jumping began to worry the few original inhabitants. . . . Whenever a newcomer attempted to squat on land already claimed, he was promptly warned, and if he still persisted, the committee proceeded to throw his shack over the river bank into what was called the Vigilantes' Depository. This action was highly exciting at times but proved effective (p. 180).

The duties of the police during 1883 and 1884 were extremely heavy. The field of their operations had been greatly extended, and as all over the country settlers were entering in large numbers, crime was much more prevalent. During 1884 five murders were recorded, two by Indians, two by white men, and one by a negro. The hanging of the last was the first execution to take place at Calgary (p. 184).

The police also had their hands full in trying to stamp out the increasing liquor traffic. Liquor arrived in a great variety of ways: alcohol as red ink; Jamaica ginger in sacks of oats; whisky in loads of hay; a hundred devices were used to evade the law. Horrible concoctions were invented by the smugglers to make quantity take the place of quality. (p. 261).

During the summer of 1884 some two thousand settlers took up homesteads in Alberta (p. 230).

The advent of the Mormon settler in Alberta is of considerable interest. It was in the year 1885 . . . that the late President Card arrived with a small party of eight or ten Mormon families from Utah and took up land in the section south of Lethbridge now known as Cardston. Other families soon followed. . . . For a time they were looked upon with suspicion by other settlers on account of their peculiar religious and social views (p. 239).

For a year or two the Indians continued to leave their reserves . . . in search of the vanished buffalo . . . they believed they would reappear (p. 147).

The Indian trades his scalping knife for a plough.
Denny used the above for one of his chapter titles. Perhaps he didn't know that scalping was a White invention.

Missionaries and Church Leaders

Missionaries, along with the trappers, traders and law enforcers played an active role in the settlement of the west. They built churches and schools, and helped established early colonies.

They administered to the sick, settled disputes, and converted a few souls, both Native and White. Notable among those that came to Alberta were Father Lacombe, the McDougalls, Robert Rundle, Bishop Grandin, Charles McMillan, Thomas Wolsely, Father Van Tighem, and George McKillop. There were many others.

Reached the Fort early in the morning and found a Popish priest there . . . [who] had made almost a dead sweep excepting the English. When will this system of lying vanities end?
    Rundle's journal June 22, 1842

[With] Methodist ministers, and priests all preaching for them-selves the poor Indians get bewildered and they do not know what religion is best.
    Robert Rundle's candid comment on the impact of his fellow missionaries.

The Catholicks [sic] are doing all in their power against us. One of them has lately baptized 700 Indians.
    Rev. Rundle's comment re the Protestant-Catholic rivalry and distrust, 1842.

He said he had done his best to preserve . . . Indians from going over to the Romanists.
    Wesleyan missionary, Thomas Woolsey, September 9, 1855. Woolsey refers to the earlier efforts of Rev. Rundle. The Protestant-Catholic rivalry and distrust were in evidence.

If Rundle had not taught the syllabics, they [Stoneys near Pigeon Lake] would have relapsed into paganism.
    Rev. George McDougall who, here, displays scant respect for native religion. "Robert Terrill Rundle," *Alberta History,* Winter 1991.

[T]he men were freezing, although wrapped in their blankets, and also had their nostrils packed with moss. Mr. MacD. overheard them talking of the probability of their being frozen to death. We walked and partook of our meal of the day – some soup made of

flour and part of a buffalo tongue. Dogs starving and eating the ends from the sledges. At dusk we started again. Terribly cold at night and the men were so fatigued that they were falling asleep on the ice; and Mr. MacD. was afraid they would freeze to death.

Rev. Rundle on his 1842 trip to the west end of Lesser Slave Lake. He refers to George McDougall here.

Read the Bible and the Bulletin.

The slogan of Frank Oliver's Edmonton paper. Oliver (1853-1933), printer, journalist, and politician was an early settler of the town, and one who put Edmonton on the map. His first paper, a two-page weekly, hit the streets on Dec. 6, 1880. Note: the first editions were five inches by six inches.

This is God speaking, I want you to get out of that office and stay out.

Edmonton's Alec Taylor, Alberta's first telegrapher and the founder of Alberta's first telephone system, spoke those words in 1884, to an intruder on the other end of the line. The amazed intruder never returned.

You trust in God. I trust in my horse.

Francois Vielle, southern Albertan Métis scout and character who galloped his horse away from two Jesuit priests he was to guide and protect. Vielle mistook a dust cloud for a Blackfoot war party.

Bishop Grandin was a most zealous missionary and had seen hard service for the church.

Cecil E. Denny. Bishop Grandin of St. Albert Mission had many years of experience in the Mackenzie River district. On the Mackenzie River he found a large and perfect emerald, which he had made into a ring during his visit to France. With Father Scollen he established Southern Alberta's first Catholic mission at Fort Macleod.

The fact was the [typical] Catholic priest was generally the guardian of the peace, the policeman, and the judge. All came to him to seek protection.

> Father Van Tighem, was a Belgium-born priest, ordained by Bishop Grandin in St. Albert in 1883. He served in Fort Macleod, Pincher Creek and gave the first Mass in Lethbridge (then Coalbanks) in 1884. *Alberta Historical Review,* 1964.

I believe we were a bit lonesome. These philosophical studies seemed to be quite arduous out there on the banks of the majestic Saskatchewan.

> Father Van Tighem. *Alberta Historical Review*, 1964.

Boys, I have come here today to hold service. I don't want to disturb you, but if you feel inclined to serve the Lord for a short time instead of the Devil, I would be much obliged, and I am sure you will feel better for the change.

> Rev. Robertson's comment to some whiskey drinking poker players in the High River Hotel, 1886. The men reportedly rose as one, attended church, sang, "Nearer my God to Thee" – and the collection was over 30 dollars. Quoted in "Early High River," *Alberta Historical Review,* Summer 1963.

What grieves me are those who are utterly indifferent to the Lord's Day and religious worship. . . . I do like the country, and had I only a congregation to preach to I should be well satisfied.

> Rev. John Gough Brick (1836-1900) on his experience in the Peace River area (circa 1890). Brick was also a pioneer farmer in that area.

No welcoming hand took mine as, tired and travel-stained after a journey of two thousand miles, I stepped out on the platform of the depot. I felt as a stranger in a strange land. I lifted my heart in prayer.

> The 38-year-old Presbyterian Reverend Charles McKillop's 1886 arrival in Lethbridge. The ex-boxer and wrestler, often-called "the fighting parson," after spending his first night

above a Lethbridge bar, soon had fisticuffs with several locals. His reputation spread.

In very early days denominations made no difference. When a minister came, everyone went to church regardless of the denomination. But when the Anglican church was built, some hard feeling was caused by the fact that after it was consecrated other ministers were not allowed to preach there. The Roman Catholic Church was the same. Everyone helped to build the churches in the early days.

Scottish settler, Alberta, 1890s.

Albert Lacombe (1827 – 1916)

Father Albert Lacombe.
Glenbow Museum NA-19-1

Some observers consider Father Albert Lacombe as the greatest of all Albertans. His life was filled with accomplishments, leaving an interesting story for future generations to explore.

The son of Agathe Duhamel and Albert Lacombe was born in Saint-Sulphice, Quebec. He was proud of his Métis blood and culture. On June 13, 1849, the young man became an ordained priest of the Oblate Order after his studies at the College l' Assumption. After brief stays and work in North Dakota and Montreal, he offered his services to Msgr. Alexandre Taché. In 1852 the young priest moved to Edmonton. He also served in Lac Sainte-Anne and the Lesser Slave Lake region.

In 1858, Father Lacombe founded the Saint-Joachim mission in Fort Edmonton, and three years later he began plans for a new mission in Saint Albert. He was given the job as a wandering evangelizer among the Cree and Blackfoot people. Soon he was becoming a diplomat and peacemaker between the tribes. During one Blackfoot – Cree battle, the priest was wounded and was saved by Chief Crowfoot.

From 1872 – 1879, Father Lacombe displayed continued flexibility with a series of appointments: parish priest in Fort Garry, leader of colonization in Manitoba, Vicar General of Saint Boniface, and priest for many of the workers building the CPR. More importantly, perhaps, is the way he smoothed the way for surveyors and work crews who brought the railroad through Aboriginal country. In 1880, Father Lacombe became the first parish priest in the young Calgary settlement. In 1884, he founded the Amerindian School in Dunbow, a hospital on the Blood Reserve in 1893, and began a school there five years later. The busy priest moved to Pincher Creek where he lived in his beloved Hermitage of Saint Michael. In Midnapore, he organized a hospice (called the Lacombe Home) for elderly people.

The Blackfoot called him *Arsouskitsi-rarpi* or Man of the Good Heart. He persuaded the Blackfoot chiefs not to support the 1885 resistance led by Louis Riel and Gabriel Dumont. He wrote a Cree dictionary and grammar book, a Cree translation of the New Testament, and a Blackfoot dictionary.

Father Lacombe made trips to Europe hoping to encourage help for immigrants coming to western Canada. He had audiences with the Pope and Emperor Franz Joseph of Austria, among other European leaders. He presented the Pope with a Cree Indian dictionary that he made himself. Consistently he prodded Ottawa for financial support.

The remarkable peacemaker and mediator is buried in the crypt of the Saint Albert parish church. The God-fearing man is remembered for his physical courage, energy, intelligence, leadership, and integrity. He used his life to define the term 'duty'. Bullets, disease, distance and cold could not stop him.

Quotes from Father Lacombe

We climbed the hills on the southern bank of the river [at Edmonton], only to discover that three Blackfeet had been massacred by their enemies, the Cree. The scalps had been taken and the hands and feet were hanging in the trees. The surrounding snow was covered with blood. I sent Alexis back to the fort [to notify] them so that someone would come for these bodies and bury them. Under the impression of this savage hate and murder we continued on our way.

Father Lacombe, after beginning a six-week visit with the Crees. Starting January 1st, 1865, he was given the mission of roaming the prairies in an attempt to evangelize among the ever-wandering Crees and Blackfoot. He was thusly freed from his work in St. Albert. It has been claimed that the priest came to know every chief of every Stoney, Blood, Blackfoot, Piegan, and Sarcee band.

And now, off to the prairies! With Alexis, my excellent Blackfoot cook, my horses, my cart, and, my portable altar, my catechisms, some objects of piety, these made up my church and my rectory. Truth to tell, I was as happy as a Prince of the Church! My people, half of which are now Christians, in the stature of great hunters before the Lord, respected and loved me. I was as a new Moses in the midst of this new Israelite camp. We were not to be fed with the desert manna, but of the tasty prairie meat sent to us by God.

Father Lacombe beginning his work as a "travelling man of God."

The patient is at first very feverish, the skin becomes red and covered with pimples, these blotches in a few days form scabs filled with infectious matter. Then the flesh begins to decompose and falls off in fragments. Worms swim in the parts most affected. Inflammation of the throat impedes all passage for meat or drink, while enduring the torments of this cruel agony the sufferer ceases to breathe, alone in a poor shed with no other assistance than what I can afford.

Father Lacombe describing the 1869 – 1870 outbreak of smallpox among Indians. At sunrise each day he buried the dead. During the day he bent over the dying, offering the parched victims water and soup – and prayers.

The hideous corpse must be buried, a grave must be dug and the body carried to the burial ground. All this devolves to me and I am alone with Indians disheartened and terrified to such a degree that they hardly dare approach even their own relations. God alone knows, what I have had to endure merely to prevent these mortal remains being devoured by dogs.

> Father Lacombe additional description of the horror. [Perhaps it is time for historians to note that the smallpox scourges were pivotal dates in Alberta's history. It has not been done extensively or well]

Well my friends, I have some advice to give you today; let the whites pass on your lands; firstly these whites who are on your land are only workers who are obeying their chiefs, and it is with these chiefs that you must settle your difficulties. I have told them of your dissatisfaction and in a few days the Lieutenant Governor himself will come.

> Father Lacombe talking to the Blackfoot Indians who understandably feared the coming railroad near their reserve, 1883.

That was a beautiful day, my audience at the Vatican. . . . How good and lovable is the Pope. . . . We talked about the Ruthenian question .

> During Father Lacombe's trip to Europe he obtained a private audience with the Pope. The visit to the continent was intended to lighten the load of immigrants coming to western Canada.

A man of eighty-six cannot expect to do very much. . . . Many years ago I stood here on this piece of ground and pictured to myself the time when a great cathedral would stand here. . . . I shall not be with you very long now. I want to plead with you for the poor and the needy and the destitute. God bless you all, both now and in your day of need and suffering. God bless you for your kindness to those needy ones at Midnapore. God bless you, people of Calgary, God bless you!

> Part of Father Lacombe's speech at his last public appearance.

Quotes on Father Lacombe

There is a wee bit of jealousy amongst these good fathers as to the popularity of Father Lacombe with the outer world. In truth, for one who has heard Bishop Grandin's name, a hundred have heard of Father Lacombe and of his influence over the Indians and the way he exerts it.

Lady Aberdeen's observation while on her 1895 visit to St. Albert. Other observers suggest that Father Lacombe out-shone his Catholic colleagues and Protestant ministers of the time.

Father, where are your decorations? You must wear them to impress the emperor.

Fifty years ago I was decorated with this [his large crucifix]. It is the only decoration I have – the only decoration I need.

Conversation between Countess Zichy and Father Lacombe who was to visit the aging Austrian emperor, Franz Joseph, September 24, 1900.

. . . guess he'll never go back to the Indian lodges after this.

This was a comment made about Lacombe after his European trip. He went back to work among his aboriginal people without hesitation. *Fifty Mighty Men*

On December 16 the old missionary's body was taken up his 'dear hill' where in the St. Albert mission started so long ago by a fresh faced, vigorous young priest, his last ceremony, conducted by Archbishop Legal of Edmonton, a long time comrade, came to a close. At its conclusion his mortal remains, except for his heart, were laid reverently in the crypt of the church beside his bishop, the saintly Grandin. By his request, his heart had been left out on the prairies of his Blackfoot people in his last great work, the Lacombe Home for the Poor.

James MacGregor in his book, *Father Lacombe*.

When Albert Lacombe was born in Quebec in 1827, western Canada was a far off wilderness . . . when he died in 1916, the 1,000,000 inhabitants of that wilderness had divided into three provinces . . . [and] for sixty-seven years he played a leading and sometimes vital part in its success. . . . Through these adventures he had grown in stature with white men and Indians alike . . . until before his death in 1916 he had become a legend in his own lifetime.

MacGregor, *Father Lacombe*

Pere Lacome [sic] was an exceedingly intelligent man, and we found his society very agreeable. Although a French Canadian, he spoke English very fluently, and his knowledge of the Cree language was acknowledged by the half-breeds to be superior to their own.

From *Cheadle's Journal of a Trip Across Canada 1862-63.*

After a capital dinner on soup, fish, and dried meat, with delicious vegetables, we strolled round the settlement (St. Albans) with our host.

Cheadle's *Journal.*

He showed us several very respectable farms, with rich corn fields, large bands of horses, and herds of fat cattle.

Cheadle's *Journal.*

He had devoted himself to . . . the improving of the condition of his flock, had brought out at great expense ploughs . . . and was at present completing a corn mill . . . a chapel, and established schools for the half-breed children.

Cheadle's *Journal.*

Fort Edmonton, Fort Calgary, Fort Macleod and Pincher Creek all may claim Father Albert Lacombe as their own.

A protestant observer.

[In the presence of sorrowing Edmontonians,] on December 16 the old missionary's body was taken up his "dear hill" where in the St. Albert mission started so long ago by a fresh-faced, vigorous young priest, his last ceremony, conducted by Archbishop Legal of Edmonton, a long-time comrade, came to a close. At its conclusion his mortal remains, except for his heart, were laid rev-

erently in the crypt of the church beside his bishop, the saintly Grandin. By his request, his heart had been left out on the prairies of his Blackfoot people in his last great work, the Lacombe Home for the Poor.

From *Father Lacombe.*

Charles Ora Card (1839-1906)

The parents of four-year-old Charles Card converted to Mormonism, and the Card family migrated from New York to the Salt Lake region in Utah in 1856, where they joined other Mormons who, led by Brigham Young, had already made the trek.

Charles, age 16, helped with the wagon and two yoke of oxen, as well as serving as buffalo hunter for the camp.

Meanwhile, Brigham Young was proving himself to be a stern moralist and the brilliant leader of what some call a cooperative theocracy. Young stated: "Our religion is simply the truth. It is all said in this one expression – it embraces all truth, wherever found in all the works of God and man" (from *Romance of Alberta's Settlements*). He believed in the practice of plural marriage: Young had 27 wives. The leader encouraged young men like Card to become more and more active in church activities.

After arriving in Utah, the Cards settled in Farmington before moving, in 1860, to Logan. Charles attended school in Ogden while becoming more involved with church work. He proved to be a successful promoter and recruiter for his church. For five years he served as second counselor to the stake president, later becoming stake president himself. Charles also supervised the construction of the Logan Tabernacle and the Logan Temple.

Authorities descended on Charles Card because of his polygamy – a practice introduced by the churuch in 1842 and made public in 1852. One of his later wives was Zina Presendia Young Williams, a daughter of the leader, Brigham Young. The 1882 Edmunds Bill effectively made plural marriages illegal. Many polygamists were heavily fined and their children were declared illegitimate. The Mormon Church was dissolved as a corporate entity. Over 1 000 Mormons were sent to jail.

Charles intended to escape custody by heading for Mexico. However, church officials suggested that Canada might be the better choice for Card. So on April 27, 1887, eight Mormon families, including the Card family, "landed" at what later became Cardston. Charles was pleased with the area's supply of timber, coal, and water. He soon returned to Utah to encourage others to come to Canada. Within four years there were nearly 400 Mormons in the area. Church officials asked Card to stay in Canada rather than return to Utah as he had planned.

In 1888, Card and other Mormon leaders travelled to Ottawa seeking permission to bring plural families to Canada. Permission was denied.

Card was the group's spiritual leader as well as an avid supporter of Mormon immigration to Alberta. Card's encouragement led to the construction of a sawmill, a dairy, and a store, as well as the canals for their growing irrigation system. Four meeting houses and a two-story school were also built. (Today his pioneer home is a treasured spot in Cardston.) Card lent his name to the town of Cardston where he served as its first mayor. To attract more settlement in Southern Alberta, local leaders combined with the experienced Mormon leadership and the federal government to plan and build a tremendous irrigation scheme along the Milk and the St. Mary Rivers. In 1898, Charles Ora Card, turned the project's first sod.

In 1902 Card's health began to deteriorate so he was relieved of his heavy duties. He returned to Logan, Utah where he lived out the last four years of his life.

Quotes from Charles Ora Card

The following quotes are from Card's Diary. Dr. Brigham Young Card, Ora Card's grandson, assisting in the writing of his grandfather's account.

Here [near the Belly River] would be a good place to establish a mission among the Lamanites who in these parts seem to be rather lighter complected than we usually find them and seem intelligent for an uncivilized race although they are much degraded by many low lived white men that allure them to whoring.
Friday, October 22, 1886.

Bishop Zundell and myself went out into the prairie between the two rivers [Belly and St. Mary rivers] and bowed before the Lord and dedicated and invoked the blessing of God upon the land and water, and asked His preservation of the same for the benefit of Israel, both white and red.
October 24, 1886, after Ora and others left Lethbridge to examine land along the St. Mary River.

It continued to snow and rain the balance of the day and . . . I had to stay in this ungodly place [Macleod Hotel] with adulterers and ungodly men who care for nothing only filthy lucre seeming lusting after the Indian women rolling in filth daily.
Wednesday, April 20, 1887.

This evening we voted unanimously that Lees Creek was the best location at present and decided to plant our colony thereon.
Tuesday, April 26, 1887.

Many times the brethren and sisters here in exile feel they are tried almost beyond that which they can bear . . . [however] here we are permitted to live free and build up a settlement.

Sunday, May 19, 1889. Card considered himself a fugitive and a refugee.

Cheer up my boy; it requires pluck to be a L. D.[Latter Day] Saint.
Saturday, April 26, 1890. Card is attempting to cheer himself after spending his first lonely night in a wagon on his way back to Canada from his U.S.A. trip. He made frequent trips from Cardston to Utah.

> I am just a pioneer –
> Landed in the eighties here;
> And the trail seemed long to Canada by team.
> When I heard the coyote howl, and the hooting of an owl,
> Then I dreamed again my early manhood dreams . . .
>
> Song written by a member of the trek led by Ora Card.

At day-light we were saluted by the firing of anvils and the hoisting of the Union Jack – the flag of Canada.
Monday, July1, 1895.

We had an excellent first meeting, several spoke in tongues, prophecies and we had a regular Pentecostal feast and we rejoiced much.
Sunday, July 4, 1897.

John McDougall
Glenbow Archives NA 1847-1

John McDougall (1842 – 1917)

In the old Canadian west, John McDougall was one of the best-known missionaries. The son of the respected Methodist missionary, George McDougall, was to follow his father's endeavors in western Canada. In 1862,

Wesleyan Methodist George Millard McDougall, his wife Elizabeth, their sons David and John, and three daughters, became the first permanent White family at the Victoria mission, 75 miles east of Edmonton. The elder McDougall foresaw the rapid White settlement in Rupert's Land.

John married Abigail Steinhauer, a daughter of a well-known Stoney family. She died in 1871 leaving her husband with three young children. The next year, John returned to Ontario and there was ordained in the Methodist church. He married his cousin, Elizabeth Boyd. They left soon after for the Alberta foothills to open a mission serving the Stoneys. John and Elizabeth had an additional six children. For over 25 years, the McDougalls served the church in Morley – a church that still stands. George was buried near the church in 1876. He had gone hunting and never returned. His body was found a few weeks later. It is thought he either had a heart attack or froze to death.

John McDougall's reports on the whiskey trade helped to convince the Canadian Government to form the NWMP. He represented Native groups at the signing of Treaty Number Seven, and applied his signature to it. As an experienced trapper and hunter, he knew the foothill country well. He tried to get government officials to provide more land for the Stoney. McDougall believed in formal "White" education for Natives who, he claimed, must become farmers. With the disappearance of the buffalo the plight of the natives became a great concern for McDougall.

McDougall retired in Calgary in 1906 where he encouraged Natives to participate in that city's first stampede.

Quotes from John McDougall

We put our trust in Providence but kept our powder dry.
John McDougall reflecting on his early days near Fort Edmonton.

[T]he poor red man was in a fair way toward extinction, just because some white men . . . themselves the evolution of Christian civilization, were now ruled by lust and greed.

John McDougall, who packed a Bible and a gun.

I secretly took the keg, emptied it [of earlier additional water] and filled it with fresh water. Mr. O'B [Eugene O'Beirne] took great pleasure in drinking this, though the taste must have been very faint indeed.

John McDougall was known for his sense of humor.

As long as we can get buffalo within 300 miles, we would prefer buffalo steaks to barley meal.

John McDougall's comment about his experiences near Edmonton.

Love and duty laugh at storms.

We had no roast beef, nor pumpkin pie, nor plates of tempting fruit, but we had buffalo boss and tongue, and beaver tail and moose nose, and wild cat and prairie chicken and rabbit and pemmican.

The Reverend McDougall's account of Christmas in Edmonton in 1864. He was a successful hunter and travelled throughout Alberta on hunting expeditions.

He was always genial and kindly and a devoted servant of God.

Pioneer missionary John McDougall on Rev. Thomas Woolsey (1818-1894).

Give the Indian full liberty in all matters except the disposition of lands and the trafficking in intoxicants.

A strong supporter of the "reserve system" for Indians, John was a keen optimist who believed that White culture and Christianity would best serve Aboriginal needs. He also favored the idea that Natives should be allowed to continue traditional ceremonies such as the Sun Dance.

Quotes on John McDougall

John McDougall never a shrinking violet, a person with an overwhelming egotism, espoused what might be called "muscular Christianity." He was one of the West's gigantic figures.

Comments by James G. MacGregor (4, p. 86). McDougall established the first Protestant schools west of Manitoba, starting one at Victoria and a second at Whitefish Lake. His mission near Morley, a combined religious institution and ranch, served the Stony Indians.

There are three liars in the territories; the trader David McDougall's one and his reverend brother [John], the other two.

Comments from an early Calgarian who knew the brothers were very fond of tall tales. Incidentally, the brothers carved out a section of the Calgary-Edmonton trail.

[John McDougall is] a thrilling platform speaker.

Report by the *Toronto Globe* (reprint) on the popular preacher who wrote six volumes of personal memoirs.

Part III
Settlements and Vistas

Seven-eighths of British North America is doomed to eternal sterility.

Scottish historian Archibald Alison, 1792-1867, who apparently never crossed the Atlantic Ocean.

A New Year's Celebration, 1800, was described by trader James McKenzie as follows: this morning before daybreak, the men, according to custom, fired two broadsides in honour of the New Year, and then came in to be rewarded with rum, as usual. Some of them could hardly stand-alone before they went away; such was the effect of the juice of the grape on their brains. After dinner, they had a bowl of punch. The expenses of this day with fourteen men and women are 6 ½ fathoms of rum, 1 ditto wine, 1 ham, a skin's worth of dried meat, about 40 whitefish, flour, sugar, etc.

The celebration was at Fort Chipewyan, the pride of the North West Company, and often then called "the little Athens of the hyperborean regions." "Social Stratification of the fur trade," *Alberta Historical Review*, Winter 1969.

[I]n a long, flat bottom of meadow, directly opposite the entrance of the Vermilion river, which falls in on the S.A. large camp of slaves [Blackfoot] begin to whoop and halloo as we came down the hills, and appeared rejoiced to see us. We passed the H.B. Co. fort and entered on our own, where we were warmly welcomed. The canoes had been absent since the 10th of May last, journeying to and from Fort Vermilion.

Alexander Henry's account, September 13, 1808.

What a spectacle. No sound was heard perhaps but the rise and splash of the fish in the lake – a slight ripple was all that was discernible on the lake – it lay almost like a sea of molten silver &

*the stars were reflected on its glossy breast – a mirrored heaven!
It was a bright starlight night.*

Rev. Robert Rundle on Pigeon Lake, November 5, 1845. On
that date Rundle described the sky as "the most brilliant I ever
witnessed, the heavens glowed like a sea of diamonds."

*I recollect a man disobeying me and [I] struck him down flat. Also
another and I displaced his jaw.*

Trader and factor John McDonald of Garth (circa 1774-1866),
often called "the last of the Nor'Westers" who helped to
establish Rocky Mountain House. "John McDonald of Garth,"
Alberta History, Autumn 1999.

*This establishment, although honoured with the name of a fort, is
a mere post for taking care of horses, a common man or horse-
keeper being in charge of it.*

Artist Paul Kane on Fort Assiniboine, west of Edmonton,
1864.

I found coal not gold.

Nicholas Sheran, 1870, a "founder" of Lethbridge.

*The position of Inspecting Chief Factor may by some be consid-
ered a great honour . . . [but] unless the grade gives me some dis-
cretionary powers, and thereby enables one to do some good.*

Chief Factor William McMurray (1824 – 1877), after whom
Fort McMurray was named.

*I have made up my mind that not a single log of men's quarters
shall be laid till the horses are provided for, as well as a few sick
men. The men's quarters will then be proceeded with, and then the
officers.*

James F. Macleod of the NWMP referring to the force's first
fort at Fort Macleod.

*Sun River – Mr. Largent says that John Healy, Al Hamilton, and
the rest of the traders at Whoop-Up, in the British possessions, are
doing well this winter. They have a good trade with the Indians,
and no U.S. detective or spy dare invade their quiet rendezvous;*

nor is whiskey ever confiscated when it gets to that 'happy hunting ground'!
    Helena Daily Gazette, February 12, 1872.

Being now in a part of the country [near the source of the Old Man River] open to hostile attack from Bands of lawless Indians we all lay down with our arms loaded for altho' the Blackfeet and Kootanies are friendly to the English we may be mistaken for Yankees.
    Robertson-Ross Journal, September 29, 1872, quoted in *Alberta Historical Review*, Summer 1961.

What inhospitable country, that sea of mountains.
    Traveller Edward Blake's reference to Alberta's mountains, Oct. 3, 1874.

A cow was driven down on one occasion for the slaughter, and on cutting open the paunch considerable coarse gold and black sand was found in it.
    Cecil Denny on an 1875 incident which seemed to support the legend of the Lost Lemon Mine in the foothills of the Highwood Mountain Range.

[H]is horse gave out at the One Pine [Olds] . . . about seventy miles from the Elbow [Fort Calgary]. He left the horse and mail there and started on foot to cross seventy miles of bare plain . . . he had been three days without food and two nights without fire.
    An 1879 Press report on Gus Govin, mailman whose route for years took him along the Calgary-Edmonton trail. Govin survived in spite of being snow-blind. There were then only 10 or 12 White people between the two centres.

The buffalo were good judges of grass.
    George "Kootenai" Brown speaking to rancher Matthew Cochrane, circa 1881. The Cochrane Ranch Company was a huge chunk of land west of Calgary. James Walker was the manager.

*Gold was mined on this river about eighteen years ago [*circa 1863*] by a man named Charlie Love, who came from "Across the Mountains." From that time each year until 1868, when there were fifty men at work. When the river was first worked on, it yielded from $12 to $20 per day to each man, but as the rich spots were worked out the average yield became lower, until now $4 a day is a fair average. In a very favorable season, however, a year or two ago, one man took out $800.*

Edmonton Bulletin, February 23, 1881.

I crossed the Milk River not far from the Sweetgrass Hills. There was no wood there, and I had to use buffalo chips for fuel. From the Milk River ridge . . . I got a magnificent view of the mountains. I crossed the St. Mary River at Whoop-Up, and touched in succession near the historic Standoff and Slideout, and finally reached Fort Macleod.

W.F. Bredin, traveller to Alberta in 1882. He also visited Calgary, Wetaskiwin area, Battle River area, Edmonton and beyond.

The Leavings [is] a name common to many other similar places . . . those traveling along the trail . . . must take water and wood from this place, as it might be sometime before they came across [more].

Alexander Staveley Hill (1825 – 1905), early owner of the Oxley Ranch near Stavely, named after the owner. Note: the spelling was changed when the town was named.

The Sioux call the place Paquapi, meaning "a hat on his hand." . . . The name of the locality in the Blackfeet language is Ne-ye-ho – "the hat on the breast," and the Cree name Na-ye-o – "the hat on the hand."

The *Regina Leader* July 5, 1883, on how Medicine Hat got its name. There are other versions.

[It is] the opinion of all being that it [the Grande Prairie area] is far superior to any other part of the country.

William Oglivie, surveyor, 1883. Note: George Kennedy was the first resident fur trader at Grande Prairie arriving about 1880. Initially Grande Prairie referred to a large area in the Peace River region. Quoted in *Alberta History,* Autumn 1997

I would rather take my chance in the industry of farming here than in any spot on Earth either south or north of the forty-ninth parallel.
    Leonard Gaetz (1841 – 1907), homesteader and founder of Red Deer, on the parkland's potential (circa 1884).

[People let] their molehills become mountains. The first time they see a real mountain they put the molehill in its proper place.
    John Brewster, former blacksmith, who arrived in Alberta's mountains in 1887. He and his family did much to open up the mountains to visitors.

The idea largely is to draft the most worthy [prisoners] . . . offering them a most liberal remission of their sentence, as well as a free grant of land.
    Sam Bedson, warden of Manitoba's Stony Mountain Penitentiary, 1888. Bedson's annual report suggested that the Athabasca region could thusly be opened up by the prisoners.

Bedson's idea is an outrageous proposal . . . [by] making a dumping ground of the Peace River country for the criminals of Canada, that it should be converted into a second Siberia or Australian penal colony.
    Fort Macleod Gazette, February 1, 1888. Bedson's idea was dismissed.

There is in the story of Alberta alone sufficient importance, interest, romance, and picturesque humour to give room for careful study and thought and to afford scope for the most polished pen.
    Lethbridge lawyer, C.C. McCaul reported in *Lethbridge News,* November 14, 1888.

The first log shacks had mud floors covered with buffalo robes. The inside of the shacks was lined with cotton, when it could be

obtained, or sometimes with newspapers. The cotton got dirty after a while because of the dust from the coal and water leaking through the roof. . . . Later when lumber could be secured, the houses had board floors. . . . Later still, paint was available.
    Scottish settler, Alberta, 1890s.

A wooden town shut in among low, treeless rolling ground; a calling river that ran unseen between scarped bunks; barracks of a detachment of mounted police; a little cemetery where ex-troopers rested . . . It was strange beyond anything that this bold telling can suggest, opening the door into a new world. The only commonplace thing about the spot was its name – Medicine Hat – which struck one instantly as the only possible name such a town could carry.
    Rudyard Kipling (1865-1936), *Medicine Hat News,* June 1892.

Wheat from Peace River won the championship; where is Peace River?
    Comment and question from Chicago newspapers after the Rev. John Brick (1836 – 1896) won Canada's first world's wheat championship in 1893. The English-born Anglican missionary started his farming career in 1881 between Peace River Crossing and Dunvegan.

I think a stalwart peasant in a sheepskin coat, born on the soil, whose forefathers have been farmers for ten generations, with a stout wife and a half a dozen children, is of good quality.
    Clifford Sifton (1861-1929), Minister of the Interior, thought highly of these folk who became known as "Sifton's Sheepskins" and "Sifton's pets," many of whom came to Alberta. Sifton's plans ranged far beyond Canada: he advertised in the U.S. and in Europe encouraging immigrants to come to the "last best west." The Manitoban's aggressive promotion of immigration had direct impact on Alberta.

I'd rather live in hell!

Comment by an Irishman as he walked toward the Edson settlement, 1902. "Edson Settlement," *Alberta Historical Review*, Winter 1962.

When I was a small boy my job in a firefighting crew was to carry the dry sacks to the nearest slough, soak them, and then gallop back to the firefighters.

V. H. Lawrence, whose account of prairie fires is reprinted in *Alberta Historical Review*, Autumn 1970.

Can you imagine being able to hear silence? I have stood outside alone and listened – absolute quiet prevailed. It filled the air. It must have been like Garden of Eden, I think.

Alberta settler, 1903.

It had turned dark and cold. Oh my, it had turned cold. Everyone was screaming and running. Our window looked towards Frank and we thought there must have been a disaster at the mine. When Mother and I found out about those poor people we cried for a long, long time.

Miss Nettie Ware's interview with C. A. Thomson in Vulcan, Alberta, regarding her memories of the Frank slide disaster, which happened at 4:10 am April 29, 1903, when 72 000 tons of rocks buried at least 66 citizens. Nettie Ware was born to John and Mildred Ware.

Old Turtle was always rumbling a little.

An often-stated comment after the 1903 Frank slide disaster.

The Mountain that walks.

Long before the disastrous land slide, Indians appropriately so named the mountain.

The rabbits died; the lynx left; the herds of antelope starved in hundreds, the poor brutes wandering into the very settlements where they were often killed in the streets.

Kelly describing the terrible winter of 1886-87 in southern Alberta.

The Sound of Edmonton

During 3 days past, Indians are pouring in continually from all quarters – such an assemblage of Strangers, who are in general inveterate enemies and ignorant of every language except their own.

Trader Duncan McGillivary at Fort Edmonton, April 15, 1795.

At almost every other post . . . the women are often seen flirting idly about the establishments, mixing among the men at their several duties . . . but it is not so here.

Alexander Ross speaking of the difference found in Fort Edmonton, while accompanying Governor Simpson for whom a formal dance was arranged "to which all white, half-breed, Indian were invited."

The walls and ceiling are painted in a style of the most startling, barbaric gaudiness . . . making altogether a saloon which no white man would enter without a start and which the Indians always looked upon with awe and wonder.

Paul Kane's description of the "ballroom" in John Rowand's establishment. Rowand was the Chief Factor at Edmonton.

Agreeably surprised at the appearance of Edmonton; finest fort I have seen in the country.

Rev. Robert Terrill Rundle, 1840. Rundle was the first Christian missionary to reside in what is now Alberta. From 1840 to 1848, as a missionary of the English Wesleyan Methodists, he worked among fur traders and Indian tribes.

Edmonton is a large establishment . . . with forty or fifty men with their wives and children, amounting altogether to about 130, who all live within the pickets of the fort. Their employment consists chiefly in building boats for the trade, sawing timber, most of which they raft down the river from ninety miles higher up, cutting up the small poplar which abounds on the margin of the river for fire-wood, 800 cords of which are consumed every winter, to supply the numerous fires in the establishment. The employment of the women, who are all, without a single exception, either squaws or half-breeds, consists in making moccasins and clothing for the men, and converting the dried meat into pemmican.

Description of Fort Edmonton by artist Paul Kane (1810-1871).

We crossed the Saskatchewan River at Edmonton with our carts and saddle horses making some of the horses swim the River . . . we took a farewell view of Edmonton, which looked well with the old British flag floating over it.

Col. P. Robertson-Ross, commanding officer and adjutant-general of the Militia of Canada, 1870. The officer travelled the west and prepared recommendations for providing law and order. His report played a significant part in the NWMP's formation. See his diary reprinted in *Alberta Historical Review*, Summer 1961.

[There was] a murderous attack upon a small party of Blackfoot Indians (men, women and children), made by Crees, near Edmonton, in April 1870, by which several of the former were killed and wounded. . . . [T]here is now living close to Edmonton a woman who beat out the brains of a little child aged two on this occasion.

Capt. W.F. Butler quoted in the *Edmonton Trader*.

I was so impressed by the quiet beauty of the scene, with its air of prestige and permanence, its assurance of present desirable conditions.

Journalist-politician Frank Oliver's recollection of his first visit (from Winnipeg) to Edmonton, 1876.

Edmonton was then [1879] nothing but a Hudson Bay company post surrounded by a high stockade . . . [which] contained many souvenirs in the shape of leaded bullets imbedded in its walls as a remembrance of many [Blackfoot] attacks.

John A. McDougall's memory of an earlier time. McDougall (1854-1928), for 50 years, was an Edmonton booster and businessman, patron of the arts, developer, politician, and respected citizen. Note: Alberta had years of slow growth. The 1901 census reported a population of 73 021. However, immigrants poured in and by 1906, the population rose to 184 412 – as recorded by MacGregor's *Edmonton Trader*.

We have nothing like a town. . . . [T]here is the fort [and] if there was no fog you could see the Methodist chapel and parsonage and scattered houses on that side . . . [and] a few Indian tents and again a few settlers' houses up the river. This is Edmonton proper.

Anglican minister, the Rev. Dr. W. Newton, Nov 1, 1879.

Edmonton, the back door to the Yukon.

An advertisement posted during the Klondike gold rush. There was no mention that the Yukon was nearly 2 000 miles of muskeg, wilderness, and hardship from that "door."

The rush to the Klondyke by the overland route through Edmonton spelled tragedy for many a poor fellow . . . many of them were childishly ignorant of what lay before them, how or by what route they would reach their destination.

Cecil Denny.

If Edmonton gets built up into a town as is expected, the sale of lumber will then come into play.

Richard Charles Hardisty (circa 1832 – 1889), fur trader and politician who served in Rocky Mountain House, Fort Victoria (now Pakan, Alberta), and Edmonton. The HBC saw a conflict of interest when Hardisty purchased a lumber mill in 1881. Seven years later he was called to the Senate, the first senator (also, first Métis senator) from the district of Alberta. Earlier, Louis Riel had put him under house arrest in Fort Garry. His daughter, Isabella, married Donald Smith who became Governor of the HBC.

At Fort Chipewyan

The term "Fort" . . . may perhaps convey an erroneous impression to the reader's mind. An imposing array of rampart and bastion, a loop-holed wall or formidable foralice may arise before his mind's eye . . . . Built generally upon the lower bank of a large river or lake, but sometimes perched upon the loftier out bank, stands the Hudson's Bay Fort. A square palisade, ten to twenty feet high, surrounds the building; in the prairie region this defence is stout and lofty, but in the wooded country it is frequently dispensed with altogether.

Inside the stockade some half-dozen houses are grouped together in square or oblong form. The house of the Bourgeois and clerks, the store wherein are kept the blankets, coloured cloths, guns, ribbons, beads etc., the commodities of Indian trade; another store for furs and pelts . . . Then come the houses of men.

Lounging at the gate, or on the shore in front, one sees a half-breed in tassaleated cap, or a group of Indians in blanket robes or dirty-white capotes; everybody is smoking; the pointed poles of a wigwam or tow rise on either side of the outer palisades, and over all there is the tapering flagstaff.

A horse is in the distant river meadow. Around the great silent hills stand bare, or fringed with jagged pine tops, and some few hundred yards away on either side, a rude cross or wooden railing blown over by the tempest, discoloured by rain or snow-drift, marks the lonely resting-place of the dead.

Wild, desolate and remote are these isolated trading posts, yet it is difficult to describe the feelings with which one beholds them across some icebound lake, or silent river, as the dog trains wind slowly amidst the snow. Coming in from the wilderness, from the wrack of tempest, and the bitter cold, wearied with long marches, footsore or frozen, one looks upon the wooden house as some palace of rest and contentment.

Edited excerpt taken from W. F. Butler's diary.
He wrote this entry while at Fort Chipewyan.

The Sound of Calgary

Behave or I'll let Bull Head have you.

A threat made by some Fort Calgary mothers to their naughty
children. Bull Head or *Stamikso-Toosan* was a large, unattrac-
tive, and pugnacious Sarcee and Cree fighter who had his own
code of behavior. The signer of the 1877 treaty was once sentenced in Calgary to two weeks imprisonment with ball and
chain and forced labor. He was jailed for disorderly conduct
and public drunkenness.

*Calgarry [sic] – Matters at Calgarry are not very stirring. The
place has not grown for the last three or four years.*
    Edmonton Bulletin, April 2, 1882. Perhaps this was the begin-
    ning of the Edmonton – Calgary rivalry?

*Some teams came in [to Calgary] from Fort Benton, and among
other supplies they brought half a dozen boxes of apples, the first
ones that ever were seen in that part of the Northwest.*
    Engineer John F. Stevens reflecting on Calgary, 1883.

*Tea is $1 per lb., sugar 2 lbs. for $1, bacon 35¢ per lb., syrup $3
per gal., beef 20¢ per lb. There is a great opening here for a butch-
er, father could really make a fat thing . . . [part of the letter is
torn away here] . . . Oats are worth $3.40 per bushel, potatoes
$6.00 per bushel, milk 12¢ per quart; so you will form an opinion
that this is an expensive country to live in. Most of the articles will
be lower after the C.P.R. reaches here.*
    Taken from a letter by Isaac Freeze, one of Calgary's first
    merchants, to his wife in 1883. "One: off to the west (Letters
    of Isaac S. Freeze)," *Alberta History,* January 2003.

*When the Blackfoot and Sarcee have washed the war paint off
their faces.*
    James Walker's answer to the question: "When are you going
    to stop for a rest and a decent meal?" (1885). Note: Walker's
    name is practically synonymous with Calgary. James Walker
    (1848 – 1936) was a homesteader, rancher, soldier, police-

man, businessman, lumber baron, and Calgary booster. He chaired the committee that secured Calgary's incorporation in 1884.

Our first sight of this enchanting spot was one never to be forgotten, one to which only a poet could do justice.
 NWMP officer Cecil Denny admiring the area that gave rise to Calgary.

The place where we had the most trouble was when we tried to cross the streets of Calgary with a herd of half-wild horses . . . this did not go smoothly.
 Armond Trochu, Brittany-born (1857) aristocrat turned Alberta rancher and enterpriser, after whom the town of Trochu was named.

No more rotgut.
 Beer magnate, rancher, developer, veterinarian, politician, administrator, and later a founder of the Calgary Stampede, Alfred Ernest Cross (1861-1932).

The general round-up was a large one, each outfit having about 15 riders, besides the cook, night herder and horse wrangler. It looked like a formidable outfit as we rode up to the high ground in the early morning from our various camps. The captain sat in his saddle like a general and picked out the most suitable riders who knew the country. Counting off about 10 riders with each, they were instructed to ride over a certain piece of country and to bring all the [200] cattle to a certain point further ahead.
 Alfred E. Cross "The Roundup of 1887, " reprinted in *Alberta Historical Review*, Spring 1965.

Western hospitality has been defined and crystallized in your genial personality; private benevolence has received its greatest encouragement from your unselfish liberality.
 Statement on a plaque honoring Pat Burns (1856-1937), cattle king, meat packer, rancher, senator, generous citizen of Calgary, and a founder of the Calgary Stampede.

You see the girl on this side [going up a hotel stairway in a Vernon hotel]?. . . [S]he's the future Mrs. Pat Burns.

Pat Burns (1856-1937), after his first glance at Eileen Ellis who later became his wife.

Small Town Alberta Buildings – ca. 1900

Let it be confessed that the architecture of these new Western towns . . . is principally governed, in the main streets, by commericial considerations and by the exigencies of necessity. On the way from Calgary to Edmonton you can see . . . the whole process of town building. The unit is the store . . . and the store in most instances, is simply a magnified packing box.

A man sends a few carloads of lumber to a township site, gets hold of a carpenter, and the big packing-box for commodities is built. A few oblong holes are punched in for windows in the upstairs department, and . . . there are the large store-windows below. Something in the way of nice architecture might be done with the gable end of the roof, but the merchant likes to have front boarding carried up square and high to hide the roof; in fact he likes it **ugly**. A plain boarded parallelogram, reaching seven or eight feet above the ridge, strikes him as about the right thing. The spirit of competition soon attracts another merchant, and we may be very sure that he will make an effort to outdo the first man in **ugly** utility.

By and by people build houses to live in, and a hotel; and naturally the same conditions prevail. The packing-box style of architecture is established for the buildings of the early years of every settlement. The people would consider it a waste of money to employ an architect, and the packing-box style of architecture needs none. The object is to get a place to store goods, or to live in that will cost as little as possible. . . .

When the people in these towns travel and see better buildings then by degrees a better style of architecture creeps in. They begin to acquire what are called "residential streets," and the packing-box architecture gives way to something much more tolerable, so that you may see both at Edmonton and Calgary.

From McEnvoy's, *A Description of Alberta Towns About 1900.*

Sounds of Transportation

They tells us there is a Certain Gum or pitch that runs down the river in such abundance that they cannot land but at certain places.

This first recorded detail about the Athabasca tar sands was from Cree Indians and given to Governor James Knight, June 27, 1715.

I could carry, paddle, walk and sing with any man I ever saw . . . no portage was ever too long for me. . . . I have saved the lives of 10 voyageurs, have had 12 wives and six running dogs. I spent all my money in pleasure. Were I young again, I should spend my life the same way.

An old voyageur, such as the ones who travelled through Alberta. These explorers worked for the North West Company, a Scotish-run, hard nosed, and efficient enterprise well-established a century before the railway arrived.

It is the worst-made that I ever saw and is more like a trough than a canoe.

NWC's Simon Fraser describing one of his difficulties: the canoes used. His job was to find a route through the mountains to the Pacific Ocean. Those instructions resulted in two expeditions. His first (1805) had him lead a party of 20 men up the Peace River to the foot of the turbulent Peace River Canyon. His missions failed but the dangerous Frazer River is named in his honor.

The bull-whacker of the west is an indigenous production, and an exotic possessing but little vitality when he is transplanted to the east . . . his oaths are never microscopic or feeble, but resounding and polysyllabic.

Fort Macleod Gazette, July 27, 1882.

The streamer "Baroness" is coaling up for her trial run to the mouth of the Belly River.

Winnipeg Daily Times, August 13, 1883. Note: The Blackfoot knew the burning qualities of the coal that was shipped from the Lethbridge area. The Blackfoot term for coal was *Si-ko-ko-to-ki* or Black rocks.

In 1883 we floated barges from the [coal] mines early in May, had the highest water of the season of the fifth of July, and I myself went up the river in the Baroness about the tenth of August.

Sir Alexander Galt's memory of the navigational season, "The Coal Fleet," *Alberta Historical Review*, Autumn 1964.

Monday, the 2nd . . . was the first Dominion Day celebration ever held in Medicine Hat, or Leopold, as the name is to be. . . . [E]arly in the evening the wind began to blow . . . a great deal of damage was done . . . [with two] barges loaded with coal going to the bottom of the Saskatchewan.

Fort Macleod Gazette, July 14, 1883.

The whole day was a succession of sports and amusements of various kinds. There was a foot race of two hundred yards for five hundred dollars a side, and outside betting ran away into the thousands. About $5 000 changed hands on the horse races. The saloons and billiard halls raked in money by the barrelfuls; the merchants drove a thriving trade, and the whole day was a continued round of excitement . . . whiskey flowed freely, and the night was made hideous with yelling, screaming and blasphemy.

Newspaperman T.B. Bradon on the celebration in Calgary on August 11, 1883 – the day the first train arrived from the east. In two months 180 miles of track had been completed.

[The stage coach was] . . . making weekly trips between said points. Leaves the Jasper House, Edmonton, at 9 and the steamboat dock at 9:30 o'clock every Monday morning, stopping at Peace Hills [Wetaskiwin], Battle River [Ponoka], Red Deer Crossing, and Willow Creek [Olds area], and arriving at Calgary

on Friday. Returning, leaves Calgary Monday, stops at same places, and arrives at Edmonton on Friday. Fare each way $25, 100 pounds baggage allowed. Express matter 10 cents per pound. Calgary office is in H.B. Co. store.

Announcement made by Donald McLeod about the First Edmonton-Calgary route. From August 1883 to August 1891, the coach was a regular feature.

The steamer Northcote of the Winnipeg and Western Transportation Co. under the command of Captain Russell arrived [in Medicine Hat] from Prince Albert on Friday last.

Calgary Herald, August 27, 1884.

The steamboat lately launched at the Coal Banks by the North West Coal and Navigation Company was named the Baroness in honour of the Baroness Burdett-Coutts who is a large sharehold-er in the company.

Fort Macleod Gazette, July 14, 1885.

But when they (Red River carts) went out a hundred or two hundred at a time . . . like ten thousand devils filing saws . . . like the shrieking damned.

An Alberta pioneer discussing early transportation.

"Alberta" Jim was busy for two days helping to round up the strayed herd [of oxen] while we made holiday, greased our wagons and braided whips.

"Alberta" Jim's story was reprinted in the *Macleod Gazette*, November 22, 1901. The unknown author refers to an 1880s incident involving a bull train.

They [voyageurs] are not brave [and] they are deceitful, and exceedingly smooth and polite, and are gross flatterers to the face of a person, whom they will basely slander behind his back. . . . men who can fight a good battle.

Daniel Harmon on the often dirty and profane voyageurs whose strength, stamina, and tenacity were as much a part of their character as their ability to work a deal any way they could.

The Finest Hotel on the North American Continent.
After railroad magnate William Van Horne renamed siding 29 "Banff," he could advertise across the world. The CPR would bring in those early tourists.

Billy Cochrane of High River has introduced the first automobile into Alberta.
High River's *Eye Opener*, 1902. Note: Two years later there were 40 automobiles in Alberta.

Why should I go to bed every night? Sleep is only a habit.
Cigar chomping, whiskey loving William Van Horne often called "The Master of the Impossible." He was largely responsible for pushing the railway across Alberta and through the Rockies.

Part IV – Expressions

Booze

The love of Rum, is their first inducement to industry, they undergo every hardship and fatigue to pro- cure a Skin full of this delicious beverage, and when a Nation  *becomes addicted to drinking, it affords a strong presumption that they will soon become excellent hunters.*

Duncan McGillivray reported in his 1794-95 journal that Nor'Westers believed the drunken Natives were "jolly hunters."

Scores of thousands of buffalo robes and hundreds of thousands of wolf and fox skins and most of the best horses the Indians had were taken south into Montana, and the chief article of barter for these was alcohol.

Methodist missionary John McDougall on the liquor trade with southern Albertan Aboriginals. McDougall lobbied Ottawa for a police force.

A man's life was worth a horse, and a horse was worth a pint of whiskey.

Recollection of an Edmonton journalist of the whiskey trade.

Raw alcohol was usually imported and the trader, once it was safely cached in Alberta, proceeded to lengthen his stock by mixing it with water, bluestone, and tobacco. Instances of men being killed by the last draught from such kegs were not at all rare.

Observation by Cecil Denny, NWMP.

I'll fix up "coffin varnish" so strong, you'll be able to shoot an Injun through the heart, and he won't die till he's sobered up.
John Healy, founder of Fort Whoop-up, boasting to Issac Baker, a Montana liquor supplier.

[At Whoop-Up] the trader stood at the wicket, a tub full of booze beside him, and when an Indian pushed a buffalo robe through the hole, the trader handed out a tin up full of some poisonous concoction. A quart of the stuff bought a fine pony.
NWMP officer, Sam Steele.

There were so many Indians at the Fort [Edmonton] that Mr. Hardisty thought I had better have evening prayers in the Hall. It was a heavy service. Indians clamorous for liquor.
Wesleyan missionary Robert T. Rundle (1811-1896) writing in his journal, February 5, 1842.

The fiery water [liquor] flowed as freely . . . as the streams running from the Rocky Mountains, and hundreds of poor Indians fell victims to the white man's craving for money, some poisoned, some frozen to death whilst in a state of intoxication, and many shot down by American bullets.
Oblate missionary Constantine Scollen on the whiskey trade's impact on the Blackfoot.

I am happy to report the complete stoppage of the whiskey trade throughout this section of the country.
NWMP's James F. Macleod smug report to Ottawa.

There were 88 Blackfoot Indians murdered in drunken brawls among themselves [in one year].
Lt. Col. Patrick Robertson-Ross reporting to Prime Minister Macdonald on the situation near Fort Whoop-Up, 1872.

We soon learned that compulsion will not make people sober. Liquor was brought in by every conceivable trick. Eggshells were emptied of their contents and alcohol substituted, [and] tin imitations of the Holy Bible were filled with intoxicants and sold.

Here, Steele reflected on the failures and successes of the (temporary) prohibition movement in Calgary and area. *Forty Years in Canada.*

Sounds of Hunters, Trappers & Traders

During the whole of the three days it took us to reach Edmonton House we saw nothing else but these animals [buffalo] covering the plains as far as the eye could reach, and so numerous were they, that they impeded our progress, filling the air with dust almost to suffocation.

Paul Kane, explorer-artist who toured western Canada (circa 1840).

Red River hunters (who hunted as far west as the Rocky Mountains) killed 652,000 buffalo in one year.

Henry Youle Hind (1823 – 1908), a naturalist and geologist who travelled to the west in 1857 and 1858. His travels and writing increased the interest of the potential of the great north west of Canada.

Wolfing was a real business in those days, when wolves could be seen in droves of 200 to 300, following buffalo herds.

Al Wilkins speaking of the 1870s. *Great Falls Tribune*, 1934.

There [near Edmonton] we passed Christmas of 1872, and one of our tidbits was a chunk of wolf-fat each. Thanks to my strychnine bait I had got three large gray wolves . . . and ate it as a relish with our leaner buffalo meat . . . I could take a large chunk of wolf fat and not only eat it, but enjoy it.

Donald Graham (1848 – 1944), Scot-born hunter who came from Manitoba to central Alberta in 1872-73. Graham's colorful letters and descriptions of life on the plains are of great value to historians. *Waiting for the Light.*

We woke to find the countryside covered with buffalo.

NWMP Constable E. H. Maunsell on the Milk River Ridge, 1874. By 1879, the buffalo were not to be seen.

Some of them took to the wilds like fish take to water. Others should have stayed home.

Jimmy Simpson, guide to the "pilgrims" (hunters), hated modern, soft life, feared for the water supply, and loved the Alberta mountains. The Stoney Indians gave him the name *Nagham-egen* meaning "wolverine-go-quickly."

When you are among wolves, howl.

NWC/HBC tracer Colin Robertson, a proud and combative Scot who was fired by the NWC after a fight with a colleague. The above quote neatly expresses the way he operated in the fur trade business.

Buffalo were still within reach on the plains to the southward and conditions were fairly prosperous.

Frank Oliver, 1876. Three years later, buffalo were gone from the Canadian prairies.

Rules of the Hunt

No buffalo to be run on the Sabbath day.
No party to fork off or go ahead without permission.
No person or party to run buffalo before the general order.
Every Captain with his men, in turn, to patrol the camp and keep guard.
For the first trespass against these laws, the offender to have his saddle cut up.
For the second offence, the offender's coat is to be taken and cut up.
For the third offence, the offender to be flogged.
Any person convicted of theft, even to the value of a sinew, to be brought to the middle of camp and the crier to call out his or her name three times, adding the word "thief" at each time.

These 1840 Métis rules were to apply to all areas of the west, including Alberta. Hunts organized in the Red River region often came to Alberta as far west as the Rocky Mountains. In one kill, 2 500 buffalo and 1 089 000 pounds of meat resulted in enough to give 200 pounds to every adult and child in the district.

It was slightly up-grade for the train, which was running about 15 miles an hour . . . but he [buffalo] made good time up hill . . . and anyone who sported a revolver produced it . . . a perfect fusillade being kept up from the train.

"A Buffalo Hunt On the CPR," *Alberta History*, Summer 2002. The anonymous account tells of the "sport" when a train west of Medicine Hat chased a single buffalo running parallel to the track. The wounded animal got away. One wonders how such a buffalo appeared as late as 1883-84.

Characters & Pioneer Humor

Whenever beef steak was to be cooked for breakfast, Jack usually prepared it by tossing it upon the kitchen floor and jumping on it with his long boots, and then throwing it against the walls or ceiling before putting it in the frying pan.

Lethbridge's John D. Higinbotham's description of the cooking talents of ex-NWMP officer, Jack Symonds, circa 1883.

The trouble, yer riverence, is he won't come back when he's sober.

Medicine Hat's Irish washerwoman, Slippery Annie, to a minister who ordered her and her boyfriend from the church because both were drunk – in spite of her fancy purple dress and his white vest, silk hat and frock coat. "Before 1905," *The Albertans.*

I'm the first white woman in the west.

Medicine Hat's other washerwoman, known as Nigger Molly. Molly and Annie were hard drinking, quick tempered rivals.

Dear Friend: My partner, Will Geary, got to putting on airs and I shot him and he is dead. Your potatoes are looking well.

Fort Whoop-Up resident "Snockum" Jim in an 1873 letter to a Fort Benton friend.

Oh, your Majesty! I have often heard of you.

High River rancher and storyteller Fred Stimson after he attended Queen Victoria's Jubilee in 1877. Simson's tall tale tells of a telephone call from the Queen, the arrival of her carriage drawn by four white horses, his visit at the palace and throughout London – and getting back to the palace at 3 am – and the Queen letting him in with her latchkey.

There were three bucks, three squaws and half a dozen children and the whole of them were actually gaunt with famine. One of the young bucks, naturally a strong, hearty lad, had an arm no thicker than my wrist. . . . Well, I gave them something to eat, not roasts especially, because they might get too fat, but parts that white men don't usually eat, and the Indians just warmed the meat by the fire and bolted it whole.

Fred S. Stimson, Manager of the Northwest Cattle Company, *Calgary Herald*, February 12, 1885. His comment, condescending and abusive, mirrored the prevailing attitude held by many Whites toward Aboriginals.

[Wetaskwin has] 287 souls plus three total abstainers.

Journalist and humourist Bob Edwards who started his weekly newspaper, the *Eye Opener*, there.

The management has decided on the name Eye Opener *because few people will resist taking it. It will run on a strictly moral basis at one dollar a year. If an immoral paper is the local preference, we can supply that too but it will cost $1.50.*

Humorist and newspaper editor Bob Edwards in the first issue of his paper, March 4, 1902. After Alberta's 1905 confederation, Edwards' Calgary paper went on to remarkable success. His genius was in his wit.

Put up your money, Doctor. I'm betting ye a dollar there is another and here's my money.

Caroline "Mother" Fulham, keeper of pigs in downtown Calgary, after the doctor treated her and commented on her unwashed and filthy leg. The man of medicine had exclaimed that "By George, I'd bet there's not another leg in Calgary as dirty as that one." Mrs. Fulham then displayed her second filthy leg. To feed her pigs Mrs. Fulham, surely one of

Calgary's great characters, would gather scrap foods thrown out by local restaurants to feed her pigs. She was known as the "Queen of Garbage Row." Frequently she was in trouble with the police who, too often, were the target of her sharp Irish tongue.

Caroline "Mother" Fulham, a well-known character in the late 1800s lived in a small cottage in Calgary where she kept a herd of livestock. A completely liberated woman, she would drink with the men and match them drink-for-drink. She was frequently in trouble with the law and local lawyer and fellow Irishman, Patty Nolan

Sketch of Mother Fulham. *Glenbow Archives NA-2240-4*

always defended her. Nolan probably enjoyed the comic melodrama in the Court Room.

Ye pur fools, what makes ye think my pur old Nellie could read your signs?

Caroline Fulham to railway officials who claimed that the lady's cow, Nellie, killed on the railway tracks by a train, was not their responsibility because a "No Trespassing" sign had been put in place.

An' it's an ill-used woman I am this day.

Mother Fulham, the "unvarnished" keeper of pigs, complaining that police had treated her roughly for at least a dozen years before her 1904 departure.

This morning she [Mrs. Fulham] got in her buckboard and the wheels came off after the horse had gone a few yards, so she knew the men had taken the nuts.

Calgary Herald, September 1, 1903. It is not known if the men were the same pranksters who painted her pigs green on a St. Patrick's night in Calgary.

I eat their livers raw.
Claim by John "Liver Eating" Johnson, a whiskey trader who allegedly killed 20 natives in hand to hand combat – and then scalped the victims and ate their livers. Johnson helped to found Fort Spitzee in southern Alberta.

[I'm ready to] fight anything from a grizzly bear to a circular saw.
Johnny Healy of Fort Whoop Up (near present day Lethbridge), Irish entrepreneur, adventurer, and prospector. Quote from *Pirates and Outlaws of Canada 1610-1932*.

The following quotes are from Denny's book.

Harry Taylor . . . brought a billiard table all the way from Fort Benton, and built a hall, which was also used for dances [in Fort Macleod].

Twenty other people are using it and it's good enough for them.
Fort Macleod hotel owner, Harry "Kamoose" Taylor to a complaining customer who asked for a clean towel.

Damn good soup, your Lordship.
Taylor to distinguished guest who asked what kind of soup was available at Taylor's establishment.

This is not London.
Harry Taylor to a customer complaining of dirty sheets, lack of door keys, and very cold water in the Fort MacLeod Hotel

Fort Macleod Hotel House Rules – circa 1888

1. Guests will be provided with breakfast and dinner but must rustle their own lunch.
2. Spike boots and spurs must be removed at night before retiring. Dogs are not allowed in the bunks but may sleep underneath.
3. Candles, hot water and other luxuries charged extra, also towels and soap. Towels changed weekly.
4. Insect powder for sale at the bar.
5. Crap, Chuck-Luck, Stud-Horse Poker and Black Jack games are run by the management.
6. Indians and Naggers – charged double rates. Special rates to Gospel Grinders and the Gamblin Profesh.
7. Every know fluid (water excepted) for sale at the bar.
8. A deposits must be made before towels, soap or candles can be taken to the rooms. When boarders are leaving, a rebate will be made on all candles or parts of candles not burned or eaten.
9. Two or more persons must sleep on one bed when requested to do so by the Manager.
10. No more than one dog allowed to be kept in each room.
11. Baths furnished free down at the river, but bathers must furnish their own soap and towels.
12. No kicking regarding the quality or quantity of food . . . Assults on the cook are strictly prohibited.
13. Quarrelsome or boisterous persons . . . and all boarders who get killed will not be allowed to remain in the house. When guests find themselves or their baggage thrown over the fence, they may consider they have received notice to quit.
14. Jewelry and other valuables will be locked in the safe. This hotel has no such ornament as a safe. The proprietor will not be accountable for anything.
15. In case of fire, the guests are required to escape without unnecessary delay.
16. The bar in the annex will be open day and night. Day drinks 50¢ each; Night drinks $1.00 each. No mixed drinks will be served except in the case of death in the family. Only regularly registered guests will be allowed the privilege of sleeping on the Bar Room floor.
17. Guests without baggage must sleep in the vacant lot until their baggage arrives.
18. Guests are forbidden to strike matches or spit on the ceiling, or to sleep in bed with their boots on.
19. No cheques cashed at any time. In God we trust all others pay cash.
20. Saddle horses can be hired at any time of the day or night, or the next day or night if necessary.
21. Meals served in rooms will not be guaranteed in any way. Our waiters are hungry . . .
22. To attract the attention of waiters or bellboys, shoot a hole through the door panel. Two shots for ice water, three for a deck of cards and so on.
23. All guests are requested to arise at 6 a.m. This is imperative as the sheets are needed for tablecloths.
24. No tips must be given to waiters or servants. Leave them with the proprietor and he will distribute them if it is thought necessary.
25. Everything cash in advance. Subject to change: board and lodging $50.00 with wooden bench to sleep on. B & L $60.00 amonth with a bed to sleep on.

The NWMP were charged with stamping out the trade in liquor. The traders resented this, particularly one very vocal man named Harry "Kamoose" Taylor (*Kamoose* means Squaw Thief). He frequently accused the police of stealing his buffalo coats. He moved from Fort Whoop Up to Macleod and opened a hotel there.

Pioneer Women

Jean-Baptiste, you heard me. I am your wife. Where you go, I go. Now say no more.

Marie-Anne Lagimodiére (1780-1875) to her husband who claimed it was too dangerous for her to travel to western Canada in 1807. Her third child, Josette, born near Fort Edmonton, was the first known White baby in what became today's Alberta. She also had the first White babies in Manitoba and Saskatchewan. Later she had great faith and love for her grandson, Louis Riel.

Tell him that I will not sell my child, and that my heart would have to be torn out before I would part with him.

Marie-Anne Lagimodiére (neé Gaboury) telling her husband what to say to a Blackfoot Native who wanted to trade two horses for Marie-Anne's little fair-haired, blue-eyed boy. Earlier the Blackfoot's wife had kidnapped the boy but his mother mounted a horse and chased the kidnapper down. Only later did the male Blackfoot, who liked the boy, come by to make the trade near Edmonton. Quoted in W.J. Healy "The First White Women of the West" in *Builders of the West: A Book of Heroes.*

Our [1874] trip from Edmonton to Morley took thirteen days. We had little comfort and freedom from worry and terror; we had only our cheerfulness to keep our courage and help us along. It was 50 below zero when we left Edmonton and I had my first baby of a year old with me.

Annie McDougall[12], wife of trader David McDougall and sister-in-law of the Rev. John McDougall. *Alberta History,* Summer 1998.

Colonel Macleod had brought up Mrs. Macleod and Inspector Winder and Sub-Inspector Shurtliff had also been joined by their wives, so now there were three ladies in [Fort Macleod} barracks. These ladies all came by way of the Missouri River to Fort Benton . . . to Macleod . . . [It was] proof of great courage on their part.

From *The Law Marches West.*

This is the first marriage of a white couple recorded at Whoop-Up. Such is the progress of civilization.

The *River Press* in Fort Benton noted the 1877 marriage of Joseph McFarlane and Miss Marcella Sheran.

We had the honour this evening of having Sitting Bull's nephew to supper in our tent. He is on his way to Ottawa. He is a splendid looking fellow and well educated. Speaks excellent English and is in every way a perfect gentleman . . . and carries a revolver at his side.

---

[12]Two women, Mrs. James Macleod and Mrs. David McDougall signed treaty Number Seven as witnesses.

Mrs. John F. McDougall in a May 25, 1879 letter written during her trip to Edmonton.

I . . . long for a woman to come and live near me. I have made all sorts of offers to a few of the men . . . of helping them to get their shacks done up if only they will go east and marry some really nice girls.

Mary Ella Inderwick who, with her husband Charles, moved 22 miles north-west of Pincher Creek in 1884. Her diary clearly describes the culture of the ranch land. "A Lady and Her Ranch." *The Best from Alberta History*

At last at 1:30 p.m., July 26, 1885, here we were in Calgary; an immense crowd at the invitation of Father Lacombe was waiting for us at the station. Father and some of his parishioners made us get into a cart and conducted us to our convent, which is about 300 yards from the railway. The bell sang out joyfully.

Notes from the 1885 Annals of the Faithful Companions of Jesus – sisters who had taken the train from Qu'Appelle to Calgary.

About March [1891] when all the ground was very dry, a terrible prairie fire broke out far to the west . . . the country was very thinly settled and in an event like that every man and sometimes women turned out to do their part. . . . The noise of the roar of the flames was so great that it sounded like hundreds of wagons rattling along.

Mrs. Ernest G. May (née Eliza Mary Paice) quoted in *Alberta Historical Review*, Winter, 1958.

Can Bab ride yet? Bab must ride if she ever wants to leave the house as one cannot walk any distance, especially a woman, on account of the cattle.

Pincher Creek Rancher's note to England regarding the pending arrival of his sister and mother, 1895. "The Reins In Their Hands," *Alberta History*, Winter, 2004.

It was a period of dry years and consequent business depression, and though the country had a fascination for us young people it was an isolated life with all the difficulties of hard work, prairie fires threatening the range, and the struggle to grow garden crops in spite of a very limited water supply, late or early frosts, sudden hail storms, and the depredations of gophers, pocket mice and jack rabbits.

Comment by Marion Moodie, first nurse to graduate in Alberta, quoted in "Marion Moodie," *Alberta History*, Winter, 2001.

The first class [of patients] were ranchers and cowboys who had broken a leg at the cattle round-up.

Nurse Mary Ellen Birtles, Medicine Hat, 1890. Birtles served Medicine Hat until 1892, then served as matron of Calgary General Hospital from 1894 to 1896. The Yorkshire-born nurse was awarded the Order of the British Empire in 1935. *Alberta History*, 1995.

The bread was fried and, of course, it was hard as wood . . . it was so hard you could knock a cow down with it.

Recollections of a male pioneer on his wife's cooking.

They [whore houses] were invariably established before the churches and long before the schools. And, if they did not actually lead the railway constructors across the prairies, they were in business long before the first trains were rolling down their new tracks. . . . Also, they [the Mounties] followed a policy of taking action only when the activities of the whores got boisterously out of hand. The West became overrun with brothels for the same reason that it broke out in a rash of boozeries – the first tides of immigration were composed overwhelmingly of unattached young men in the prime of life. . . . There were three times as many brothels alone as there were churches.

James H. Gray, *Red Lights on the Prairies*. Gray's book deals with the problem of prostitution in early Drumheller, Lethbridge, Edmonton, and Calgary, among other western centres.

White Slaver
If a report speaks truly there is one man at least in Lethbridge who deserves something only a little less than hanging. It seems that a certain individual of this town, a short time ago induced a young girl from across the line to make the journey to Lethbridge in the hopes of securing a good situation. On her arrival here, however, the victim was promptly taken to a house of ill-fame. Fortunately, a report of the transaction reached the ears of a gentleman who succeeded in rescuing the girl and placing her in a respectable household.
Lethbridge News, March 2, 1898.

The population of the North-West would be rapidly and materially increased by a few more such women.
Press comment after the 36-year-old wife of Lethbridge's William Stafford gave birth to her twelfth child.

[I] made the usual mistake of bringing out a maid from home; but [later] I took to the broom and duster, and was surprised to find what a calmness descended on my spirit with release from the task of supervision.
Poetess Moira O'Neill (pen name, Mrs. Walter Shrine, 1864 – 1955) who lived near High River for six years shortly after her 1893 marriage.

Our imports are easily enumerated. A little flour, occasionally, is a treat, rice and raisins, sugar, tea, salt, and spice constitute about the slim total. A can or two of peaches found their way here last summer. We also have some dried apples; but I can assure you the produce or our country is not to be despised. I like barley bread very well; we have also excellent butter, our own manufacture. The potatoes and turnips, I fancy, taste better than they did in Ontario. Fish and rabbits constitute the chief living of the poor man here, both of which are very plentiful nearly all the year round. They put down nets under the ice, even now, and the fish caught are very superior.
Diary of Elizabeth Barrett (circa 1841 – 1888), an articulate and talented Ontario-born teacher and poet who began her

A Pioneer School Teacher

Dec. 24, 1862: As I suppose Your Lordship is aware that the Company refused to give any assistance, I need not say anything on that head. Although the people in the fort are only poor, yet they were very glad to have an opportunity of supporting a school. . . . I take my meals in Mr. Cunningham's house, and . . . he sends his four boys to school free of charge.

I began to teach about the end of September, and although the boys did not know even the alphabet there are many of them now reading. Mr. Christie has acknowledged that they have learned more during the two months that I have been here then [sic] in two years with Mr. Wolsely, the minister. I suppose Father Lacombe will ask for the books that are necessary for next year.

. . .

Apr. 30, 1863: There are two children at the mission whose father was murdered by the Black-feet [sic] . . . they are Indians of the Stoney tribe. My boys are learning English pretty fast now; most of them can read and write. . . . Mr. Christie and the people of the fort are all very glad to have a school for their children. I should be very glad to receive a few school cards for beginners, if there are any to spare at the Red River College. If there is also a terrestial globe to spare, it will be very useful to me here to give explanations to the boys.

. . .

Jan. 7, 1864: We had examination in the school a few weeks ago; it was attended by Rev. F. Lacombe, Mr. Christie . . . [they] seemed well pleased. . . . After the examination, Mr. Christie gave the boys a very encouraging lecture.

. . .

Dec. 29, 1864: The more I teach these poor little children, the greater love I feel for them and the greater is my desire to see them advance rapidly in their studies. My pupils are 30 in number.

In 1862, a young Irishman named Constantine Scollen arrived at Fort Edmonton and opened a school for the children of White and half-breed employees at the post. He was the first qualified Roman Catholic teacher in the area and came as a lay brother for the Oblates.

The above excerpts of letters written from Fort Edmonton to Bishop Tache at Red River (now Winnipeg) during his first three years as a teacher. The *Mr. Wolsley* he mentions is Reverend Thomas Wolsley, the Methodis missionary; *Mr. Christie* is William Christie, chief factor at the fort; and the *Company* is the Hudson's Bay Company.

western work at White Fish Lake near Lac La Biche in 1875. Later she taught at Morley and Fort Macleod. Quoted in *Alberta History*, Autumn 1998.

Our houses were made of hewn spruce logs mostly. We had only two windows in them, no upper floors, no glass, but a rawhide skin of a deer or moose calf was used . . . it was put on the window while wet . . . [so] no Peeping Tom was going to peep through your window.
    Victoria Callihoo (1860 – 1966), (née Belcourt) married to Louis, son of an Iroquis chief, and farmer at Villeniuve. Her account is found in *Alberta Historical Review* (reprint), n.d.

We had no soap, but we made a potash from fats and grease with ashes lye. We used it for our toilet and washing soap. Perhaps it was rather hard for the delicate skin.
    Victoria Callihou, quoted in *Alberta Historical Review* (reprint), n.d.

I awoke one morning during the first week of May, 1902. . . . I carefully shook the snow off the bed covers, for a light skiff had fallen during the night and some of it had found its way through the unfinished walls of the house.
    Anna McNellis in "A Woman's View of Pioneer Life," *Alberta History*, Summer 1954

Silence of Death

    Because of their isolation, Native populations of North America had no immunity to numerous diseases that had ravaged Europe for years. In the 1830s, a steamboat arrived at Fort Union on the Yellowstone River with two men on board having small-pox. In a short time, the disease spread. By the late 1830s, smallpox outbreaks wiped out large numbers of Blackfoot, Assiniboine, and Mandan people.

We had no belief that one man could give it to another, any more than a wounded man could give his wound to another.

A Peigan's statement to David Thompson (1770-1857), surveyor, explorer, map maker, and fur trader after witnessing the awful deaths caused by smallpox. Approximately 50 percent of Alberta's Aboriginal population died in the 1869-70 epidemic.

Not a sound can be heard to break the awful stillness, save the ominous croak of the ravens, and mournful howl of wolves fattening on the human carcasses that lie strewed [sic] around. It seems as if the very genius of desolation had stalked through the prairies, and wreaked his vengeance on everything bearing the shape of humanity.

A frightened traveller's account of the results of the 1837 smallpox epidemic brought to Rupert's Land by traders returning from the Missouri River area of Montana. Thousands of Natives and a few Whites were victims.

They [Blackfoot] wanted to see if they would get the smallpox [from the liquor] and when they found out they did not, they opened trade with us. I got 108 buffalo robes and nine horses for the keg of rum.

James Gibbons, trader and minor, circa 1869. The town of Gibbons, just north of Edmonton, was later named in his honor.

It is a hard thing to bury our own dead.

David, son of missionary George McDougall, after burying family members, victims of the 1870 smallpox epidemic near Pakan.

It was late in the fall of 1870. The preceding year, smallpox had swept through the Blackfoot tribes and left in its wake whole camps of dead lodges, the mortality rate being estimated by competent authorities at forty or fifty per cent.

Dr. G. A. Kennedy, *Lethbridge Herald,* April 30, 1890. About 50 percent of Alberta's Aboriginals died in the 1869-70 smallpox epidemic. Official figures for the Saskatchewan district show that 2 686 Plains Natives, 485 Cree, and 373 Métis died of smallpox.

The population of St. Albert is stated at 800; of this number 320 died [from smallpox] at the colony or out in the plains.
The Manitoban, January 21, 1871, on the 1869-70 outbreak.

Formerly they had been the most opulent Indians in the country, now they were clothed in rags, without horses or guns.
Father Constantine Scollen on the Blackfoot tribe after the 1869-70 smallpox epidemic.

I shall have to make a big cut. If you all do as I tell you after the big cut is made, this man may get well, but I cannot tell for sure until I have made the big cut, and then if he does not get well, and if he should die, you must not blame me. . . . Shall I make the big cut?
Pioneer Lethbridge doctor, Frank Hamilton Mewburn, to the family of a sick Blood Indian in 1885. The rather frail, hot-tempered doctor operated on the man's severe goiter. Memburn's first Native patient recovered completely.

Political Voices

There was a man who would always fight for what he considered the right. They couldn't buy him, and they couldn't scare him.
Admirer of "Honest Frank" Oliver (1853-1933), politician and founder of the *Edmonton Bulletin*. He was a member of the North-West Council (1883-1885) for Edmonton. Later he served in the NWT Legislative Assembly before serving as Minster of the Interior under Wilfred Laurier.

Boy, you have too good a head to be a carpenter. Why don't you take up the law?
Lawyer and Sunday School teacher Samuel Blake of Toronto to James Lougheed (later Sir James), who became a pioneer, lawyer, developer, Calgary booster, businessman, senator –

and grandfather of an Alberta Premier. James Lougheed was the first and only Albertan to be knighted (1916). In 1883, he witnessed the arrival to Calgary of the first CPR train.

King Apow wishes to speak to you.
A messenger telling Norman Luxton, perhaps Banff's most famous son, that a Native king of a South Pacific island wanted to see him immediately. The king said: "You will marry my daughter and live here." The fearful Albertan agreed. All night dancing and drinking of cava followed the 1901 mar-

> Oliver rides on white horses,
> Cochrane on a mule,
> Oliver is a gentleman,
> Cochrane is a fool.
>
> Words of a song sung by some Alberta children regarding the Liberal Oliver and the Conservative Cochrane, 1896.

riage. Luxton, a world traveller, publisher, and a founder of Banff Indian Days had Calgary's Luxton Museum named in his honor.

That boy'd make a good Westerner.
Senator James Lougheed on the young New Brunswick-born lawyer, R.B. Bennett, who arrived in Calgary in 1897. Bennett, then called the "Boy Orator" later became Prime Minister.

Resolved, that in the opinion of this Board, the time has fully arrived that calls for this portion of the Dominion of Canada, known as the North-West Territories, to be erected into a Province, with all Provincial rights and privileges. The great number of settlers pouring into the Territories from all parts of the world, the greatly increased demands for money for roads, bridges and public works, as well as schools, most strongly impress upon the Board that the only successful way to cope with and meet our ever-increasing obligations is by having the power to deal with all the vast requirements of this portion of Western Canada from the standpoint of a Province.

> Resolution (similar to others from Alberta) of the Calgary Board of Trade, March 3, 1903.

The filling up of the North-west with settlers is not merely a question of furnishing a market for the manufacturers and the traders of the east. It is not merely a question of filling that country with people who will produce wheat and buy manufactured goods. It is a question of the ultimate result of the efforts being put forward for the building up of a Canadian nationality, so that our children may form one of the great civilizations of the world, and be one of the greatest forces in that civilization.

> Frank Oliver, M.P. (Lib) Alberta, House of Commons, July 14, 1903.

Sir Frederick William Haultain.
From the Saskatchewan Archive Board.

Sir Frederick William Haultain (1857 1942)

Alberta and Saskatchewan were created as provinces in 1905. The efforts of the scholarly English-born Fort Macleod lawyer, Frederick William Alpin Gordon Haultain, were largely responsible. In 1883, the young Ontario-educated Haultain took the stagecoach south to Fort Macleod from Calgary. He fell in love with the area and its people.

Haultain was elected to the first Legislative Assembly of the North West Territories and later became virtual Premier of the area. Although Haultain was the Premier, Ottawa, through the Lieutenant Governor, largely controlled the area. Haultain led the group that demanded responsible government for the Territories. He also argued that the west's geography suggested no natural line for the political division of what became Alberta and Saskatchewan. Haultain proposed that the larger province should be named Buffalo.

Many experts believe that Haultain should have been named Premier of one of the new provinces. When the Edmonton and Regina inauguration ceremonies took place Haultain was nowhere to be found.

Later, Haultain was knighted, named Chancellor of the University of Saskatchewan, and named Chief Justice of that province's Court of Appeal.

Many observers believe that Frederick Haultain, son of Fort MacLeod, continues to be underestimated by Canadians.

Quotes from Sir Frederick William Haultain

The Territories have arrived at a point where, by reason of their population and material development, the larger power and larger income of a province become necessary.

I am more convinced than ever that there is no necessity for dividing the country into two provinces with the consequent duplication of machinery and institutions.

Let us call our province Buffalo.

Quotes on Sir Frederick William Haultain

The man with the best claim to statesmanship was conspicuously absent.

Biographer Grant MacEwan, commenting on Haultain's failure to attend the 1905 inauguration ceremonies in Edmonton (Sept. 1) and Regina (Sept. 4).

If Frederick Haultain had had his way, Alberta and Saskatchewan would never have been split in two.

Aritha van Herk, historian, University of Calgary, 2005.

Part V – Alberta Particulars

What's in a Name?

In March, 1871, Princess Louise Caroline Alberta, the Queen's fourth daughter and purportedly the most attractive one, married the Marquis of Lorne at St. George Chapel in Windsor Castle. The couple moved to Kensington Palace, where Queen Victoria had been raised.

The princess has been described as outgoing, pampered, vivacious, and sometimes as imperious as her mother. Her husband, John (Marquis of Lorne and later ninth Duke of Argyll) was a quiet, reflective, rather guileless, quick-minded man, an observer rather than a doer. The marriage produced no children. There were rumors surrounding Lorne's alleged homosexuality and that the princess never menstruated. Tongues wagged.

The couple moved to Canada in 1878 when the British Prime Minister appointed Lorne the Governor General of Canada. Lorne's love of Canada blossomed. He particularly loved the west and was thrilled by Fort Calgary. When he later joined his wife in England he found it "dark and unwholesome" compared to Canada's "bright light and the dry and beautiful snow with its sapphire colored shadows."

Lorne later felt that his life and marriage required his resignation as Governor General. The couple returned to Britain where Lorne had plenty of time to pursue his writing career and care for his estates in Scotland. Often, Lorne and Louise went their separate ways.

In 1882, Lorne named the earlier provisional District of Alberta in honor of Princess Louise Caroline Alberta who probably never visited the province herself. The Governor General wrote the following:

In token of the love which thou has shown
For this wide land of freedom I have named
A province vast and for its beauty famed.
By thy dear name to be hereafter known.
Alberta shall it be. Her fountains thrown
From Alps unto three oceans, to all men
Shall vaunt her loveliness e'en no: and when
Each little hamlet to a city grown.
And numberless as blades of prairie grass
Or the thick leaves in distant forest bower
Great peoples hear the giant currents pass
Still shall the waters, bringing wealth and power
Speak the loved name – the land of silver springs
Worthy the daughter of our English kings.

In 1905 the newly created province was also named after the princess.

Alberta Vernacular, 1880s Style

The following expressions, among others, are suggested by John D. Higinbotham in "Western Vernacular," *The Best from Alberta History*, Dempsey, 1981. In 1884, Higinbotham (1864-1961) opened the west's first drugstore in Fort Macleod.

- That pony is not large as a bar of soap after a hard day's washing.
- That old hoss is too dead to be buried.
- When yer lost, yer 40 miles from nowhere.
- He was so cross-eyed that his tears ran down his back.
- That hoss needs a new hackamore (rawhide or horse hair halter).
- Go sleep on your goose hair (feather tick or pillow).
- He snaked my cache (stole my hidden money).
- Them coal miners got hearts so small you could pak 'em in a mustard seed.
- It's dead nuts (inevitable) that he'll lose the fight.
- We got dough-gods (dumplings), sow-belly (pork) or rattle-snake (bacon) for grub.
- Yesterday, we had tent-pegs (beef cut into strips), baked wind-pills (beans), and paperweights (hot biscuits) with dope (butter) for grub.
- Last night the NWMP arrested another keg angel (whiskey trader).
- We call our whiskey: coffin varnish, pizen, rot-gut, bug-juice, red-eye, tangle-foot, and a lot more.
- Are you goin' to the blowout (party or dance) tonight?
- Them hymn-howlers, gospel grinders, devil-dodgers, sky pilots – call them missionaries how you like – are tryin' to corral me.
- That thief need the hemp-line route (hanging) to the great hereafter.
- She'd down to the bedrock (poverty stricken).
- Her husband was first a bull worker (bull train driver) and later a mule-skinner (mule train driver).
- I carry my equalizer (gun) every time I hit Calgary.
- She just hits the ground in the high places (rides a horse fast).

From Kerr D. G.G.'s, *A Historical Atlas of Canada*.

Alberta Timeline to 1905

- **1670** King Charles II of Britain grants the territory of Rupert's Land to the Hudson's Bay Company.
- **1754** Anthony Henday of the Hudson's Bay Company arrives in present-day Alberta.
- **1793** Alexander Mackenzie crosses present-day Alberta on his way to the Pacific.
- **1794** Hudson's Bay Company fort built at present-day Edmonton.
- **1807** Fort at Edmonton is destroyed.
- **1819** Fort at Edmonton is rebuilt and serves traders and missionaries.
- **1821** The North West Company merges with Hudson's Bay Company.
- **1832** John Rowand takes charge of Edmonton House.
- **1840** Rev. R.T. Rundle, Methodist, takes up residence in Edmonton.
- **1852** Father Lacombe arrives.
- **1854** John Rowand dies.
- **1857** Palliser Expedition arrives.
- **1861** Father Lacombe establishes St. Albert.
- **1862** Arrival of Rev. George McDougall.
- **1868** Hudson's Bay company sells Rupert's land to the new confederation of Canada for 300 000£ sterling ($1 460 000 Canadian).
- **1869** Canadian Parliament adopts an act for the temporary Government of Rupert's Land and the North-Western Territory when united with Canada, which establishes an advisory council of members selected by Ottawa.

  First whisky post – Whoop-Up – built.
- **1870** Smallpox epidemic.

- **1871** The advisory council is formed to make recommendations to the lieutenant-governor.

- **1872** Canada's Dominion Lands Act offers immigrants a 160-acre homestead in the West for $10 and allows ownership of the land after three years if certain conditions are met.

- **1874** Northwest Mounted Police establish Fort Macleod in southern Alberta.

- **1875** Northwest Mounted police build log fort at present-day Calgary.

  Canadian Parliament adopts the act to amend and consolidate the laws respecting the Northwest Territories to separate the lieutenant-governor of Manitoba from the lieutenant-governor of the Northwest Territories and to establish a new advisory council with greater powers.

  The new advisory council has members elected by districts of populations greater than 1 000.

  The advisory council becomes a legislative assembly when the council consists of at least 25 members.

- **1877** Treaty Number Seven signed with the Blackfoot.

- **1882** District of Alberta is created and named in honor of Queen Victoria's daughter whose husband is governor-general of Canada.

- **1883** Canadian Pacific Railway builds through Alberta.

  Alberta elects first representative to Territorial Government.

- **1885** Northwest Territories elects four members of Parliament, including D.W. Davis for the Alberta constituency.

  The first senators for the Northwest Territories are named.

  The Canadian government sends military personnel to Calgary as part of the move against Louis Riel.

- **1888** Richard Charles Hardisty is appointed to the Senate of Canada as the first senator from the district of Alberta and is Canada's first Métis Senator.

- **1889** Northwest Territories is administered by a legislative assembly which held certain powers such as taxation, issuing permits, establishing municipalities, managing court and local company incorporations, and the ability to spend money from taxes; the lieutenant-governor is authorized to spend money from the Canadian government.

- **1890** Crowfoot dies.

- **1891** Canadian Parliament amends the Northwest Territories Act, 1875, so the Legislative assembly recommends expenditures of all public funds and forms an executive committee whose members take an oath of office and receive a salary.

- **1896** Canadian Minister of the Interior, Clifford Sifton, advertises in Europe for immigrants, offering free acres to settlers.

  People from Germany, the Ukraine, and Romania respond to Sifton's offer.

  Father Lacombe starts St. Paul des Métis colony.

- **1897** Canadian Parliament makes extensive changes to Northwest Territories administration, leading to responsible government of the people. An executive council replaces the executive committee. Government departments are created. However, the Territories cannot borrow money, cannot obtain revenues from public lands which are administered by Ottawa, cannot tax the CPR according to the charter, and monies are not enough to pay for the schools and other public services that are required for the increasing population.

  Frederick William Haultain becomes president of the Executive Council, earning him unofficial role of Premier of the Territories.

- **1898** Edmonton serves as supply base during the Klondike gold rush.

- **1900/01** Prime Minister Laurier meets with F.W.G. Haultain and J.H. Ross of the Territories to discuss territorial self-government.

- **1903** Frank Slide.

- **1904** As federal Parliament is dissolved, Laurier promises to resolve the issues in the Territories if he is re-elected.

- **1905** Alberta becomes a province.

  The Canadian government refuses to give Alberta control of its own resources, resulting in a 25-year feud in part because the Canadian government wanted to retain control of immigration policies for the prairies

Bibliography

Alberta History. Calgary: Historical Society of Alberta, 1994 - 2004.

Alberta Historical Review. Calgary: Historical Society of Alberta, 1954-1970.

Autobiography of John Macoun, Canadian Explorer and Naturalist, 1831-1920. Ottawa Field-Naturalist's Club,. 1979, Second Edition.

Belyea, Barbara Ed. *A Year Inland: The Journal of a Hudson's Bay Company Winterer*. Waterloo: Wilfrid Laurier University Press, 2000.

Betke, Carl Ed. *Alberta Album: The Living Past*. Edmonton: Lone Pine Publishing, 1985.

Bruce, Jean. *The Last Best West*. Toronto: Fitzhenry & Whiteside, 1976.

Burpee, L.J., Ed. *York Factory to the Blackfeet Country – The Journal of Anthony Henday, 1754-1755*, RSCT, 3rd series, Vol I, 1907.

Butler, William Francis. *The Great Lone Land 1910*. Edmonton: Hurtig Publishers, reprint 1968 (1).

———— *The Wild North Land 1915*. London: Burns and Oats, 1915 (2).

———— *Forty Years in Canada*. Toronto, Herbert Jenkens Ltd., 1915 (3).

Callwood, J. *Portrait of Canada*. Markham: PaperJacks Ltd., 1983.

Canada West Magazine (1981-1993). Currently *Canada West: The Pioneer Years*. N.L. Barlee, Summerland BC. Stagecoach Publishing.

Chalmers, John W. *Fur Trade Governor: George Simpson 1820-1860*. Edmonton: Institute of Applied Art, 1960.

Cheadle, Walter B. *Cheadle's Journal of a Trip Across Canada 1862-63*. Ottawa: Graphic Publishers, 1931 (reprint).

Clutton-Brock, Elizabeth. *Woman of the Paddle Song*. Toronto: Copp clark Publishing, 1972.

Colombo, John Robert. *Colombo's Canadian Quotations*. Edmonton: Hurtig Publishers, 1974 (1).

———— *Colombo's New Canadian Quotations*. Edmonton:Hurtig

Publishers 1986 (2).

———— *The Dictionary of Canadian Quotations*. Toronto: Stoddard Publishing, 1991 (3).

———— *Famous Lasting Words*. Toronto: Douglas & McIntyre, 2000 (4).

Cruise, David & Griffiths Alison. *The Great Adventure: How the Mounties Conquered the West*. Toronto: Penguin Books, 1997.

Denny, Cecil E. *The Law Marches West*. Cameron, W. B., Ed. Toronto: JM Dent & Sons, 1939 (reprint).

Dempsey, Hugh A., Ed. "Black White Man," *Alberta Historical Review*. Calgary: Historical Society of Alberta, 1958 (1).

———— Ed. *The Best of Bob Edwards*. Edmonton: Hurtig Publishers, 1976 (2).

———— Ed. *The Rundle Journals 1840-1848*. Calgary: Historical Society of Alberta, 1977 (3).

———— Ed. *Charcoal's World*. Saskatoon: Western Producer Prairie Books, 1978 (4).

———— "Death of a Son," *Western Profiles*. Edmonton: Alberta Education, 1979 (5).

———— *Jerry Potts, Plainsman*. Calgary: Glenbow Institute, 1980. (6)

———— *Red Crow: Warrior Chief*. Lincoln & London: University of Nebraska Press, 1980 (7).

———— Ed. "A Lady and Her Ranch," *The Best from Alberta History*. Saskatoon: Western Producer Prairie Books, 1981 (8).

———— Ed. "On the Plains in 1872-73," *Waiting for the Light*. Saskatoon: Western Producer Prairie Books, 1981 (9).

———— "The Snake Man," *Alberta History*. Calgary: Autumn 1981 (10).

Deyell, Edith. *Canada: a New Land*. Toronto: W.J. Gage Ltd, ca 1970.

Dickie, Donalda. *The Great Adventure:* Toronto: J.M. Dent & Sons

Earl of Southesk. *Saskatchewan and the Rocky Mountains*. Edinburg: Edmonton and Douglas, 1875.

Fardy, B. D. *Jerry Potts, Paladin of the Plains*. Langley: Mr. Paperback, 1984.

Ford, Theresa M. *Western Profiles*. Edmonton: Alberta Education, 1979.

Francis, Daniel, and Payne, Michael. *A Narrative History of Fort Dunvegan.* From www.bigthings.ca.

Francis, R. Douglas et al. *Origins.* Toronto: Holt Rinehart and Winston of Canada Ltd, 1988.

Gillese, J. P. "Before 1905," *The Albertans.* Edmonton: Lone Pine Publishing, 1981.

Godfrey, D. G. & Card, B. Y. *The Diaries of Charles Ora Card: The Canadian Years 1886-1903.* Salt Lake City: University of Utah Press, 1993.

Grain Growers Guide. Sept. – Dec. 1918 (Photocopy).

Gray, James H. *Red Lights on the Prairies.* Toronto: Macmillan of Canada, 1971.

Green, Larry. "John McDonald of Garth," *Alberta History.* Calgary: Autumn 1999.

Hamilton, Jacques. *Our Alberta Heritage.* Calgary: Calgary Power Ltd, 1977.

Hamilton, Robert M., & Shields, D. *The Dictionary of Canadian Quotations and Phrases.* Toronto: McClelland and Stewart, 1979.

Harmon, Daniel Williams. *Sixteen Years of Indian Country.* Ed. W. Kaye Lamb. Toronto: Macmillan Company of Canada, 1805.

Hopwood, Victor, Ed. *Travels in Western North America 1784-1812.* Toronto: MacMillan Canada, 1971.

Horwood, Harold & Butts, Edward. *Pirates and Outlaws of Canada 1610-1932.* Toronto, New York: Doubleday, 1984.

van Herk, Aritha. "Imagine One Big Province," *Canadian Geographic.* Jan. – Feb, 2005.

Kane, Paul. *Wanderings of an Artist Among the Indians of North America.* Edmonton: MG Hurtig Ltd., 1968 (reprint).

Kelly, L.V. *The Range Men: The Story of Ranchers and Indians of Alberta.* Toronto: William Briggs, 1913.

Kerr, D. G. G., Ed. *A Historical Atlas of Canada.* Toronto: Thomas Nelson & Sons, 1961.

Lamb, W. Kaye, Ed. *The Journals and Letters of Sir Alexander Mackenzie.* London: Cambridge University Press, 1970.

MacEwan, Grant. *Fifty Mighty Men.* Saskatoon: Modern Press, 1959 (1).

———— *. . . and Mighty Women Too.* Saskatoon: Western Producer Prairie Books, 1975 (2).

MacGregor James G. *Father Lacombe.* Edmonton: Hurtig Publishers, 1975 (1).

———— *Senator Hardisty's Prairies 1840-1889.* Saskatoon: Western Producer Prairie Books, 1975 (2).

———— *John Rowand: Czar of the Prairies.* Saskatoon: Western Producer Prairie Books, 1978 (3).

———— *A History of Alberta: Revised Edition.* Edmonton: Hurtig Publishers, 1981 (4).

———— *Behold the Shining Mountains.* Edmonton: Applied Art Products Ltd., 1954 (5).

———— *Edmonton Trader: The Story of John A. McDougall.* Toronto: McClelland and Stewart Ltd., 1963 (6).

McDougall, John. *Pathfinding on Plain and Prairie.* Toronto: William Briggs, 1898 (reprint).

McEvoy, B. *A Description of Alberta Towns about 1900: From the Great Lakes to the Wide West.* Toronto: William Briggs, 1902.

McGillivray, Duncan. *Journal. Ed. by A.S.Morton.* Toronto: University of Toronto Press, 1929 (reprint).

Newman, Peter C. *Caesars of the Wilderness: Company of Adventurers. Vol. II.* Markham Penquin Books Canada Limited, 1987 (1).

———— *Company of Adventurers.Vol. I.* Toronto: Markham Penguin Books Canada Limited, 1986 (2).

Owram, Douglas, Ed. The Formation of Alberta – A Documentary History. Calgary: Alberta Records Publication Board, Historical Society of Alberta, 1979.

Pitt, S. "Beware the Windigo," *Legion Magazine,* January/February, 2003.

Rasmussen, Linda et al. *A Harvest Yet to Reap: A History of Prairie Women.* Toronto: Women's Press, 1976.

Rodney, William. Kootenai Brown – His Life and Times. Sidney, BC: Grayay's Publishing Ltd., 1969.

s

Shipley, Nan. *The James Evans Story*. Toronto: The Ryerson Press, 1966.

Silversides, B.V. *Waiting for the Light*. Saskatoon: Fifth House, 1991.

Sealey, D.Bruce. *Jerry Potts*. Don Mills: Fitzhenry and Whiteside Ltd, 1980.

Steele, Samuel B. *Forty Years in Canada*. Toronto: Hebert Jenkins Ltd., 1915 (1).

————— "Wild and Wooly Days," *Great Canadian Adventures* Montreal: The Readers' Digest Association, 1976 (reprint) (2).

Stevens, J. R. *Sacred Legends of the Sandy Lake Cree*. Toronto: McClelland & Stewart, 1971.

Strickland, David. *Quotations from English Canadian Literature*. Toronto: Modern Canadian Library, 1973.

Thomson, Colin A. *Blacks in Deep Snow*. Don Mills: J.M. Dent & Sons Ltd., 1979 (1).

————— *Swift Runner*. Calgary: Detselig Enterprises Ltd., 1984 (2).

—————*The Romance of Alberta Settlements*. Calgary: Detselig Enterprises, 2004 (3).

—————*The Romance of Alberta Settlements*. Calgary: Detselig Enterprises, 2004 (3).

Titley, Brian. *The Frontier World of Edgar Dewdney*. Vancouver: UBC Press, 1999.

Turner, J. P. *The North-West Mounted Police 1873-1893*. *Vol. I*. Ottawa, King's Printer, 1950., 1965.

Titley, Brian. *The Frontier World of Edgar Dewdney*. Vancouver: UBC Press, 1999.

Turner, J. P. *The North-West Mounted Police 1873-1893*. *Vol. I*. Ottawa, King's Printer, 1950.

Wagner, Henry R. *Peter Pond, Fur Trader and Explorer* [New Haven]: Yale University Library, Radisson and Des Grosilliers, 1955.

Index

Alberta, Princess 159, 160

Antrobus, Sergeant W.D. 54

Barrett, Elizabeth 150

Bedson, Sam 123

Bennett, R. B. 155

Birtles, Mary Ellen 149

Bishop Zundell 114

Brown, George Kootenai 56-59

Butler, William Francis 48-51

Fidler, Peter 15-18

Card, Charles Ora 112-114

Hardisty, Richard 64, 129, 164

Harmon, Daniel Williams 23-25, 135

Harvey, Alexander 51

Haultain, Frederick 156-158, 165

Healy, John 120, 138

Healy, Johnny 144

Hector, James 34, 39

Henday, Anthony 7, 9-13, 163

Henry, Alexander 119

Higinbotham, John 66, 141, 162

Hill, Alexander Stavely 122

Hind, Henry Youle 139

Holmes, Mrs. Robert 68

Inderwick, Mary Ella 148

Ings, Fred 92

Irvine, A.G. 63, 64

Jarvis, William 90

Jasper House 31, 39, 47, 61, 134

Johnson, John "Liver Eating" 144

Judge Scott 94

Kane, Paul 120, 126, 127, 139

Kennedy, George 81, 123, 153

Kipling, Rudyard 124

Knight, Governor James 133

Lacombe, Father Albert 70, 73, 79, 81, 103, 106-112, 148, 151, 163, 165

Lagimodiére, Marie-Anne 146, 147

Laurier, Wilfrid 7, 154, 165, 166

Lawrence, V.H. 125

Leduc, Father Hippolyte 75, 77, 79

Lesser Slave Lake 31, 37, 67, 68, 79, 104, 106

Lethbridge 8, 52, 53, 62, 64, 68, 80, 93, 102, 105, 106, 114, 120, 123, 133, 141, 149, 150, 154

Livingstone, Sam 91, 92

Longbaugh, Harry 92

Lougheed, James 86, 88, 154, 155

Love, Charlie 122

Lt. Gov. Archibald 51

Lt. Gov. Edgar Dewdney 63, 71

Lt. Gov. Laird 50

Luxton, Norman 155

Lynch, Tom 83

Macdonald, John A. 70, 73, 138

MacEwan, Grant 69, 70, 157

MacGregor, James 67, 73, 110, 111, 118, 128

Mackenzie, Alezander 14, 163

MacLeod, James F. 52, 53, 54, 65, 68, 70, 94-98, 120, 138, 147

Macoun, John 42-43

Marquees of Lorne 159

Maunsell, Constable E.H. 140

May, Mrs. Ernest G. 148

McCaul, C.sC. 123

McDougall, Annie 147

McDougall, David 118, 147

McDougall, George 103, 104, 115, 153, 163

McDougall, John 63, 68, 72, 115-118, 137, 147

McGillivary, Duncan 126

McKillop, Reverend Chalres 105

McLeod, Donald 135

McMurray, William 120

McNellis, Anna 152

Medicine Pipe Stem 93

Mewburn, Frank 154

Mills, Dave 80, 81

Mills, Harry 89

Moodie, Bill 83

Moodie, Marion 149

Newton, Reverend Dr. W. 128

O'Neill, Moira 150

Oglivie, William 123

Oka, Mike 89

Oliver, Frank 65, 90, 104, 128, 140, 154, 156

Palliser, John 33-36, 62

Parker, Robert Le Roy 92

Pond, Peter 13-15

Potts, Andrew R. 51

Potts, Jerry 51-56, 68, 96, 98

Poundmaker 71, 72

Queen Victoria 26, 49, 141, 157, 164

Red Crow 63, 65, 68

Reid, Jim 77, 78

Reverend Robertson 105

Richard, Edouard 7

Riel, Louis 49. 52, 68, 98, 107, 129, 146, 164

Robertson, Colin 140

Robertson-Ross, Col. P. 127, 138

Ross, Alexander 33, 126

Rowand, John 30-33, 126, 163

Rundle, Robert 61, 62, 103, 104, 120, 126, 138,

Scollen, Constantine 104, 138, 151,154

Seton, Ernest Thompson 42

Sgt. Wilde 93

Sheran, Nicholas 120

Sifton, Clifford 124, 165

Simpson, George 25-30, 31, 80

Simpson, Jimmy 140

Slippery Annie 141

Snockum Jim 141

St. Albert (Grand Lac) 50, 104, 105, 108, 110, 111, 154, 163

Stafford, William 150

Steele, Sam 54, 65, 91, 93, 138, 139

Steinhauer, Henry Bird 67

Stevens, John F. 130

Stimson, Fred 85, 141, 142

Stuart, John 29

Swift Runner 74-79

Symonds, Jack 141

Tache, Bishop 151

Taylor, Alec 104

Taylor, Harry 144

Thompson, David 18-23, 153

Trochu, Armond 131

Turnor, Philip 16, 17

"Twelve Foot" Davis 36-38

Van Horne, William 136

Van Tighem, Father Leonard 103, 105

Vielle, Francois 104

Wachter, Fred 89

Walker, James 121, 130

Ware, Amanda 85, 125

Ware, John 80, 82-85

Wentzel, Williard 29

Wilkins, Al 139

Williams, Dan 35, 81

William, Jesse 85-87, 91
Windigo 74, 75, 79
Wolseley, Garnet 49
Woolsey, Thomas 103, 117